THE ECONOMICS OF NATIONAL FOREST MANAGEMENT

Marion Clawson

E 70 ?

Resources for the Future
Washington, D.C.

June 1976

RFF WORKING PAPER EN-6
DISTRIBUTED BY THE JOHNS HOPKINS UNIVERSITY PRESS, $4.50

Resources for the Future is a nonprofit organization for research and education in the development, conservation, and use of natural resources and the improvement of the quality of the environment. It was established in 1952 with the cooperation of the Ford Foundation. Part of the work of Resources for the Future is carried out by its resident staff; part is supported by grants to universities and other nonprofit organizations. Unless otherwise stated, interpretations and conclusions in RFF publications are those of the authors; the organization takes responsibility for the selection of significant subjects for study, the competence of the researchers, and their freedom of inquiry. This book is a product of RFF's Institutions and Public Decisions Division, directed by Clifford S. Russell.

This material has been published without the usual editing and typesetting in order to speed its distribution.

Library of Congress Catalog Card Number 76-15939
ISBN 0-8018-1889-3

RFF Working Paper EN-6 $4.50

PREFACE

This working paper is an expression and an outcome of my interest in forest economics. That interest has been long existent, but it was greatly stimulated by my experience as a member of the President's Advisory Panel on Timber and the Environment, in 1971 to 1973. It became evident to me during that period that the potentialities of American forests were very imperfectly realized. In the past two years I have been able to give further expression of that concern in the RFF book, Forest Policy for the Future: Conflict, Compromise, Consensus, which I edited and to which I made some written contribution, and in the RFF book, Forests for Whom and for What?, which I wrote.

This paper concentrates upon the management of the national forests. The analysis herein tries to consider, as far as available data will permit, all outputs of the national forests, considering that each kind of output is equally valid, but that each must unavoidably be valued in economic terms. Likewise, as far as incomplete data permit, it considers all costs of national forest management, including particularly capital costs (interest), which in practice are the greater part of national forest costs. As long as man's means are limited in relation to his wants -- which is almost certainly, forever -- then economizing as a process is unavoidable. Some things can be chosen, others cannot; some are possible but simply too costly in relation to values. In focusing on economics here, I do not intend to imply that economics is the only perspective from which to examine forests. It is, however, a neglected aspect of national forest policy analysis and one with enormous implications.

At the beginning, let me emphasize as strongly as I possibly can that in my analysis: economics does not mean only timber, and economics does not mean only values which are captured in dollar terms.

i

This paper has been written with a broad audience in mind. First of all, it is addressed to the users of the national forests and, when one takes into account the dependence of every one of us upon wood fibers in some form for housing, furniture, and paper in all its forms, that means every citizen of the United States. I am talking also to the professional foresters in public and in private employment, for I think the analysis in this book could offer them new insights and new challenges about forest management. I am talking to public officials, federal and state, including those in the Congress and in state legislatures, because I think my analysis may offer them potentials for better meeting the needs of their electorates. I am talking to the fine men and women of the Forest Service, even if, or perhaps especially as, I am being critical of national forest management. If a better future is to be achieved with the national forests, they must play a major role in its achievement. And, I am talking to the forest industry, because such a large segment of it depends upon timber bought from the national forests.

I particularly urge conservationists, recreationists, wildlife lovers and specialists, wilderness advocates and buffs, and the preservationists to read this paper, and to ponder on the facts and analyses contained herein. I think this study could offer them much. In the past, many of them too often considered economics as their enemy. I think they should reconsider their position. At the very least, they should be fully aware of the economic potentials and parameters of national forest management. In my judgment, an approach based upon the economics developed in this paper will do more to help these interests attain what they want from national forests, than will exclusively emotional appeals on the values of the outputs they seek.

My concern is that the national forests make their greatest possible contribution to the well-being of the American people. Well-being must be measured as the greatest excess of all values over all costs. The problems in national forest management to achieve this end include considerations of physical-biological feasibility and consequences, economic efficiency, economic equity, social acceptability, and administrative practicality, as I pointed out in my book, Forests for Whom and for What?. The problems are complex and difficult but the values are great.

It is my considered judgment, after a careful review of all the relevant evidence I could find, that the national forests today are inefficiently managed. They are wasteful in their use of capital, money is spent in the wrong places and for the wrong activities, and their economic potential is not realized. The responsibility for this state of affairs is divided, as I point out, and the Forest Service alone cannot be considered responsible for the results. I invite the reader's attention to my evidence as well as to my conclusions.

Portions of this paper appeared in Science, February 20, 1976, p. 762, under the title, "The National Forests."

This paper uses the best data available to me, and makes the best economic analyses of which I am capable within the time and resources available to me. Much of it is judgmental, in the sense that it reflects my judgments built up over a good many years, using not only the data included herein but a great deal of experience not readily reducible to footnotes. Much of this paper is critical about the economic management of the national forests. Explanations are offered as to why the record is so bad, and suggestions are made as to how a different future might be attained. The soundness of both

explanations and conclusions depends upon the evidence and the analysis. Anyone can make sweeping criticisms and offer radical proposals; criticism and
proposals which merit attention must rest upon more than personal judgments,
no matter whose the judgments may be.

I must acknowledge the help of many people, while at the same time
absolving them of any responsibility for my analyses and conclusions. I am
greatly indebted to the people with whom I worked on the President's Panel
on Timber and the Environment, to a considerable number of reviewers of the
manuscript for my book, Forests for Whom and for What?, and to many others,
too numerous to mention individually. A special word of thanks is due to
the Forest Service, for the data used in this paper. Though we often, and I
believe rightly, criticize these data for their deficiencies, they are the
best we have, and in many cases all we have, and analysts like myself are
wholly dependent upon the Forest Service for its data. I am also appreciative
of the help of some of my colleagues at RFF, notably Charles J. Hitch, Emery N.
Castle, Hans H. Landsberg, Clifford S. Russell, John V. Krutilla, and most
especially to William F. Hyde, who so often helped me out, and to Lawrence W.
Libby of Michigan State University who spent 1974 at RFF and whose work I use
directly in this paper. A draft of this report was reviewed by William B.
Bentley, of the University of Michigan, currently a Bullock Fellow at Harvard
Forest, and by Herbert Kaufman of the Brookings Institution, and their comments
were most helpful in its revision.

I am, of course, also appreciative of the competent and helpful contributions of my secretary, Blossom Carlton, and for the help of the editor,
Joan Tron.

Marion Clawson

December 1975

Washington, D.C.

CONTENTS

TABLES

FIGURES

I. The National Forests: An Overview

Introduction[1]

The national forests of the United States are a great national asset.
They include 8 per cent of the total land area of the nation, have a sale or
liquidation value estimated at $42 billion, in recent years their cash receipts
have ranged from $400 to $500 million, and their output or use directly or in-
directly affects everyone in the United States.[2] The national forests are
big business in the American sense of the term; if they were a private industrial enterprise, on the basis of their gross cash income alone in each of the
past twenty years or more they would have ranked about half way up Fortune's

---

[1] The source of much of the basic data for this report is U.S. Department
of Agriculture, Forest Service, The Outlook for Timber in the United States,
Forest Resource Report No. 20, October 1973. This source and many others
present relatively detailed data for 1970, hence this is used as the base
year for much of this report. Where significant changes have occurred in
more recent years or where data for a single year might be misleading, trend
data or averages for periods of years are used. The financial data in the
latter part relate to various years after 1970, the choice of year depending
in part upon economic conditions that year and in part upon data availability.
Use of a single year, for example, 1975, would be highly desirable but is not
possible. It is hoped that using different years does not confuse the reader.
Virtually all U.S. data for forests and forestry employ such American units
as acres, board feet, and cubic feet, hence these units have been retained
here, rather than conversion to metric units. It is unfortunate that those
anachronistic terms and concepts "sawtimber" and "board feet" have not been
replaced in practice by the concepts of "wood" and "cunits" (100 cubic feet),
respectively, for these are far more relevant to modern forestry. To permit
easier comparison with earlier and current writings about forests, I have
retained these outmoded terms and concepts in spite of my distaste for them.

[2] There is a substantial literature about national forests, some of which
is cited later. For books which present an overall view of the national
forests and the Forest Service, see: D. Barney, The Last Stand, New York:
Grossman, 1974; Michael Frome, The Forest Service, New York: Praeger, 1971;
and Glen O. Robinson, The Forest Service: A Study in Public Land Management,
Baltimore: Johns Hopkins University Press, for Resources for the Future,
1975.

list of the 500 largest industrial enterprises, and on the basis of their
capital value they would have ranked still higher. Yet the national forests
have never been really studied as business enterprises.

The national forests, as all forested areas, produce many kinds of outputs -- wilderness experiences, other outdoor recreation experiences of a more
intensive and popular kind, water, wildlife, and wood in various forms. With
rare exceptions, it is the wood harvested which produces the cash income to the
forest owner, whether that owner be a private individual or company or whether
it is a public agency. To a substantial extent, the various outputs of the
forest are joint products from a single productive resource, with all the problems inherent in joint outputs.

In a consideration of national forest management, all goods and services
produced from such forests must be considered on the income side of the equa-
tion and all costs, including capital charges (interest) on investment values
must be included on the expense side. Frequently, available data are somewhat
deficient and estimates must be made to provide data for missing items. Such
estimates cannot be precise but it is hoped they are approximately accurate
and the analysis as a whole is more accurate by the use of estimates than would
be the case if the missing items were ignored.

Most of the available data about forests and forest output apply to wood
growth and use. These data are frequently less than ideal, but the data inade-
quacies for other outputs and uses are far more serious. As a result of this
data situation and of the financial importance of wood growing, much of this
report, as any writing about national or other forests, must concentrate to a
large extent on wood growing and harvest, in spite of a desire to present a
balanced treatment of all forest uses and outputs.

1. What the National Forests Are

The national forests are a large area of land owned by the U.S. government in the proprietary sense, largely but not wholly forested, under multiple use management which considers outputs and values for wilderness, outdoor recreation, wildlife, watershed, and other purposes as well as wood growth and harvest. To understand the nature and the role of national forests in modern American life, it is necessary to consider their history briefly.

In 1891, Congress enacted the Forest Reserve Act. For many years before this, some conservationists had been much alarmed by the relatively rapid harvesting of the virgin forests of the country, where extensive fires often followed harvest, and tree regeneration was scanty or lacking. These conservationists had urged various measures upon a largely indifferent Congress. Passage of the 1891 Act had a number of aspects which cannot be explored in this article.[3] Under the Act, Presidents Harrison and Cleveland reserved some millions of acres of the public domain. Until 1897, there was little or no management of these withdrawn lands and no legal authority for their use in any way. In 1897, Congress provided authority for the use and management of the national forests (then called forest reserves) in legislation which is still basic today.

_____

3/ For discussions of the Act, see: Jenks Cameron, The Development of Governmental Forest Control in the United States, Baltimore: Johns Hopkins Press, 1929; Samuel T. Dana, Forest and Range Policy: Its Development in the United States, New York: McGraw-Hill Book Co., 1956; Paul Gates, History of Public Land Law Development, Washington: USGPO, 1968; W. B. Greeley, Forests and Men, Garden City: Doubleday, 1951; Benjamin H. Hibbard, History of Public Land Policies, New York: The Macmillan Company, 1924; John Ise, The United States Forest Policy, New Haven: Yale University Press, 1920; E. Louise Peffer, The Closing of the Public Domain, Stanford: Stanford University Press, 1951; Gifford Pinchot, Breaking New Ground, New York: Harcourt, Brace and Company, 1947; Roy M. Robbins, Our Landed Heritage, Princeton: Princeton University Press, 1942; New York: Peter Smith, 1950; Harold Steen, an unpublished history of Forest Service, tentatively titled "The Greatest Good for the Greatest Number: A History of the U.S. Forest Service."

President Theodore Roosevelt, under the stimulus of Gifford Pinchot, made extensive further withdrawals of land in the public domain for inclusion in the forest reserve system. These large withdrawals so alarmed Congress that an act in 1907 forbade further withdrawals in most western states without specific congressional approval. Roosevelt, before he signed the 1907 bill, made additional extensive withdrawals.

The gross acreage of the national forests in 1907 was about what it is today; some lands have since been restored to public domain status and thus were open to private entry, others were added. The additions were made possible by the Weeks Act, passed in 1911, which provided for purchase of private land to establish or to extend national forests. This law has been especially important in the eastern half of the country as the means of establishing national forests in this large region where little public domain land remained in 1891. In the 1930s, land was purchased under the submarginal lands program, and the administration of these lands has recently been placed in the hands of the U.S. Forest Service.

The extensive withdrawals of land in the public domain to form the forest reserves in the decades around 1900 were possible in large part because the lands involved were not in strong demand by private parties, who could have obtained them under other land laws. The forest reserves (now national forests) were typically the more remote and inaccessible areas at that time. Products and services from the national forests continued in relatively low demand until World War II. The management of the forests, until approximately that time, was primarily custodial -- to prevent fires, to suppress those that did occur, to keep trespass to a minimum, to regulate grazing, and to make modest timber sales. Forest replanting, especially on depleted forest lands purchased from private owners, also went forward in this period. Beginning somewhere around 1950, national forest management entered a new phase. It became more intensive, as demands for products and services from the national forests rose and as harvest of various outputs increased. In very recent years, management of the national forests seems to have been entering still another phase, one which may best be characterized as public-oriented. The meaning of this term, as it applies in practice, may perhaps become clearer later in this report.

Some Basic Definitions

Basic to all discussions about forests, and about national forests in particular, are the definitions of forest land and commercial timberland.

Forest land is defined as "Land at least 10 percent occupied by forest trees of any size, or formerly having had such tree cover, and not currently developed for nonforest use. The minimum area for classification of forest land is one acre. Roadside, streamside, and shelterbelt strips of timber must have a crown width at least 120 feet wide to qualify as forest land. Unimproved roads and trails, streams, or other bodies of water or clearings in forest areas are classed as forest if less than 120 feet in width."[4]

Commercial timberland is defined as "Forest land producing or capable of producing crops of industrial wood and not withdrawn from timber utilization. Areas qualifying as commercial timberland have the capability of producing in excess of 20 cubic feet per acre per year of industrial wood in natural stands. Currently inaccessible and inoperable areas are included, except when the areas involved are small and unlikely to become suitable for production of industrial wood in the foreseeable future."[5] "Industrial wood" includes wood used for lumber, plywood, pulp and paper, poles, railroad ties, and many other uses.

The definition of forest land is intentionally a broad one, in the sense that areas very sparsely occupied by trees, as well as very small areas, are

4/ The Outlook for Timber in the United States, p. 310.

5/ Ibid.

included. In the definition of commercial timberland, "withdrawn" means that areas reserved from cutting by law, such as national parks and wilderness areas, are excluded. The definition is applied to fully stocked natural stands at a point in their age-growth curve when the average annual growth rate is at or near a maximum. Actual growth may be far below this, as later sections of this report will show. No allowance is made in this or in other Forest Service land classifications for higher yields that would result from forestry more intensive than fully stocked natural stands. As noted, the definition includes areas where harvest is impractical at present and perhaps always. The definition gives no consideration to the value of the wood; one cubic foot is implicitly assumed as equal to every other cubic foot, irrespective of species or grade of log. No allowance is made for cost of harvest, including the cost of building necessary roads. The definition is a physical or biological one, not an economic one.

Although the definition of commercial timberland excludes some areas where more intensive or different management might produce more wood or more valuable wood, in general it includes a large acreage where continued forest management for wood production is not economically feasible. In later sections, we introduce data on acreages and productivity of forests by site classes. In general, and with exceptions, Site Class V forests (capable of producing more than 20 but less than 50 cubic feet of wood per acre annually) are not commercial in the sense that they can be managed economically to grow wood. Class V forests include 27 percent of the commercial forest area of the United States, but they have only 12 percent of the productive capacity for wood growing. Various adjustments in the reported commercial forest acreages and volumes can be made to include only those areas where profitable wood-growing seems probable. The extent of such adjustments would clearly change as economic conditions change.

Acreage in National Forests

Today the national forest system (including lands of all designations
under the management of the Forest Service) includes 187 million acres (Table 1).[6]
By no means all of this is forested, even by the generous definition previously
given -- some is grassland, some is above timberline, and some is bare rock.
Of that which has some forest cover, by no means all is commercial forest --
some is pinion-juniper or other sparse forest types with too low a capacity to be
considered commercial forest even by the generous definition, and some has been
eliminated from the commercial forest category by its reservation and inclusion in wilderness areas. Not quite half of the total area is classed as
commercial forest and 29 percent of this is in Site Class V. Thus the poten-
tially economically productive wood-growing lands in the national forests are
about 65 million acres -- still a large area, nearly twice as large as Iowa.

Because of their history, the national forests are predominantly in the
West -- one-third along the Pacific Coast, over 40 percent in the Rocky Mountains, and only one-fourth in the whole eastern half of the country. In the
West, about half of all commercial forest land is in the national forests; in
the East, the proportion is less than 6 percent.

Because of their regional location, and because forest types differ
greatly by regions, the national forests are far more important for their
softwood timber resource than they are for the hardwood resource (Table 2).
They include well over one-fourth of the national acreage of all softwood

6/ Of the extensive literature relating to forests in general and to national forests, the following are most relevant to the discussion which follows
this section: Marion Clawson, Forests for Whom and for What?, Baltimore: Johns
Hopkins University Press for Resources for the Future, 1975; Marion Clawson,
ed., Forest Policy for the Future, 1974; William A. Duerr, ed., Timber!, Ames,
Iowa: Iowa State University Press, 1973; G. R. Gregory, Forest Resource Economics, New York: Ronald Press, 1972; President's Advisory Panel on Timber
and the Environment, Report, Washington: USGPO, 1973; David M. Smith, The
Practice of Silviculture, New York: Wiley, 1962; Stephen Spurr and Burton
Barnes, Forest Ecology, New York: Ronald Press, 1973; Albert Worrell, Principles of Forest Policy, New York: McGraw-Hill, 1970.

Table 1. Acreage of National and Commercial Forests Compared
with Total Land Area, by Region, 1970

(millions of acres)

Region[a]	Total land area (1)	Total area of commercial forests (2)	National forests	
			Total area (3)	Area of commercial forests (4)
Pacific Northwest	470	50	45	23
Pacific Southwest	104	18	20	8
N. Rocky Mountains	215	37	48	24
S. Rocky Mountains	340	25	48	16
North	628	178	14	10
South	513	193	12	11
Total	2,270	500	187	92

Sources: Columns 1, 2, and 4: The Outlook for Timber in the United States,
Appendix Tables 1 and 2, pp. 225-230. Column 3: Robinson, The
Forest Service, pp. 289-306.

a/ The areas covered are: Pacific Northwest--Alaska, Oregon, and Washington;
Pacific Southwest--California and Hawaii; N. Rocky Mountains--Idaho, Montana,
South Dakota, and Wyoming; S. Rocky Mountains--Arizona, Colorado, Nevada,
New Mexico, and Utah; North--New England, Middle Atlantic, and Central
Census regions; South--South Atlantic, East Gulf, Central Gulf, and West
Gulf Census regions.

Table 2. Total and National Forest Acreage of Commercial Forests,
by Region and Major Forest Types, 1970

(million acres)

Region	Softwood types[a]		Hardwood types[b]		Nonstocked	
	Total	National forests	Total	National forests	Total	National forests
Pacific Coast (including Alaska and Hawaii)	55.4	28.8	8.5	1.2	3.7	0.9
Rocky Mountains	49.6	30.7	4.3	2.1	2.7	2.0
North	38.3	3.3	130.0	6.8	9.6	0.4
South	98.9	6.0	88.8	4.6	4.8	0.1
Total	242.2	68.8	231.6	14.7	20.8	3.4

Source: The Outlook for Timber in the United States, Appendix Table 46,
pp. 302-309.

a/ White, red, jack pine; spruce-fir; longleaf-slash pine; loblolly-short-
leaf pine; oak-pine; Douglas fir; ponderosa pine; western white pine; fir-
spruce; hemlock-Sitka spruce; larch; lodgepole pine; and redwood forest
types.

b/ Oak-hickory, oak-gum-cypress; elm-ash-cottonwood; maple-beech-birch; aspen-
birch; and all western hardwood forest types.

types, and nearly 60 percent of such types in the West. National forests include only 6 percent of the hardwood acreage. These acreage data emphasize
that the national forests are primarily (1) western and (2) softwood.

When Europeans first came to what is now the United States, they found
immense forests, varied as to species, rich in volume and quality of timber,
largely mature except where fire, storm, or insect infestations had recently
struck, and hence with little or no net annual growth. The history of forestry
in the United States in the past 300 years is very largely the history of the
harvest of those mature ("virgin") stands of timber. Outside of the national
forests, national parks, and a few other publicly owned areas, these stands
have, almost without exception, been influenced heavily by man's actions. Re-
peated harvests, frequent burnings, much natural regeneration, and some seeding
and planting have led to the creation of new forests. Sometimes these differ
in forest type from the virgin forest, but they always differ in the age class
of their standing trees, with lower stand volumes per acre, and nearly always
with substantially faster net growth rates than the original mature forests.

Sustained Yield as Applied to Old Growth Forests

The concept of sustained yield for forestry was developed many decades ago
in Europe, and introduced to this country nearly 100 years ago. This concept
requires that annual harvest (or harvest every few years) be limited to net
wood growth in the same period. Unless harvest is limited to growth, it would
reduce the inventory of growing stock and impair the ability of the remaining
stand to grow wood. This fact is generally realized because it is so obvious
to anyone, once it has been explained. What is not so obvious, and as a result
is often unrealized, is the fact that harvest must take place, if growth is to
be possible. Unless the trees are cut, they reach their maximum size (a mature
forest) and no more net growth is possible. The first step to growing more wood
in a mature forest is to cut the trees now standing. Cut must equal growth,

12

annually or over a very few years; cut and growth are equally dependent upon each other. Many persons not well versed in forestry emphasize the need for limiting cut to growth, but often overlook the equal necessity of cutting if growth is to be maintained.

Under a sustained yield management system, timber inventory is constant or nearly so. Sustained yield may be applied on small or on large areas. On small areas, only a few trees can be cut each year, and this generally means some form of selective cutting; on larger areas, small patches can be harvested annually by selective cutting, clearcutting, or any variant of either. By relaxing the time constraints within which cut and growth must balance, even small areas might have relatively heavy cuts some years and none in other years.

Any method of timber harvest can be conducted well or badly. The criteria for judging the quality of the harvesting method are (1) the resulting effect on the site and (2) the resulting effect upon the timber stand which remains or which develops later. It is possible to conduct a timber harvest to protect the site from erosion, to protect the water courses from siltation, to maintain the water quality, and to avoid offensive aesthetic consequences. The opposites of each of these desired results are also possible from any method of timber harvest, if the timber operator is careless or heedless. Timber harvest, even of a few selected trees, is an ecological shock to the existing timber stand. The regeneration of the timber on the site for the same or for other species may be prompt or it may be delayed, it may be of desired species or of some undesired ones, it may result in a thrifty growing stand or it may result in a poor and unthrifty one, or it may have other consequences. There are many bad examples of each method of harvesting. Some of the bad examples of clearcutting have been widely publicized, but selective cutting may as effectively destroy the productive forest as does clearcutting, although in ways less obvious to the casual observer. There is unfortunately much that

is not yet known about the silvicultural practices that would ensure the kind
of forest desired after cutting. Weather and other factors present hazards
that may make the actual outcome differ from the desired one. The appropriate
harvest method depends on the site, the species, the harvest technology, and
the comparative costs.

The application of the concept of sustained yield to mature forests is
very difficult, yet that is what the Forest Service has been trying to do for
many decades and is still struggling with. Any cut, no matter how small, in a
mature forest is in excess of net growth that year, and any system of regular
annual harvests in a mature forest will continue in excess of annual net growth
for many years. The harvest, even if small, and regardless of the method, re-
duces standing timber volume on the area cut; the rest of the mature forest is
making little or no net annual growth. Only when the net annual growth on the
previously cut areas is greater than the annual harvest will net growth exceed
harvest. Some observers of national forests have been disturbed that harvests
exceeded growth in recent years, apparently not realizing that this is an in-
escapable consequence of any timber harvest of mature stands. If a forest
manager seeks to convert a mature forest into a wood production forest, on a
sustained yield basis, the real questions he faces are: over what time period
should he spread the cut of mature timber, and how long a rotation should he
use in growing new timber.

Throughout most of the long history of exploiting the privately owned
forests of the North and South, cut exceeded growth, and many persons cried
"timber famine." Theodore Roosevelt, in his seventh annual message to Congress
in 1907, said, ". . . so rapid has been the rate of exhaustion of timber in the
United States in the past, and so rapidly is the remainder being exhausted, that
the country is unquestionably on the verge of a timber famine. . . ." He seems
to have overlooked the fact that trees grow. During the past twenty-five years

or so, the volume of hardwood timber grown in the United States annually has exceeded the annual cut, and timber inventories are being built up rather rapidly; for softwoods, cut still exceeds growth and inventories are being reduced; the overall balance is an increase.

Because of their history, the western softwood national forests are still largely old growth timber. On the Pacific Coast, nearly 80 percent of the commercial forest area in the national forests is sawtimber (and about the same proportion has over 5,000 board feet of standing timber per acre); in this same region, the forest industry has only about 60 percent of its forests in this category. In the Rocky Mountain regions, well over half the area of commercial forests in the national forests has sawtimber stands.

For those national forest lands designated for commercial timber growing, the conversion of the old growth to managed timber rotation will be a major forest management problem for the next several decades.

Site (Productivity) Classification of National Forests

Forests differ greatly in their ability to grow wood and to produce other outputs of the forest. The combination of such factors as climate, elevation, soils, location on the Earth's surface with respect to the Poles and the Equator, and other natural factors determine the kinds of trees and their annual rates of growth in forests which experience little influence by man. Even here, fire from natural causes, storms of various kinds, insects, and disease are powerful factors affecting forest type, rate of wood growth, and volume of stand at any date. The natural forces would work out to a "climax" or equilibrium forest over a period of time, but for many sites the time period must be measured in centuries. For instance, a dominantly Douglas fir forest 400 years old may not yet be the climax, because the hemlock which will reproduce in the shade may ultimately take over the site, in the absence of other disturbances which would open up the site for the Douglas fir to grow. Where man has intervened significantly by timber harvest, by man-caused fires, by fire control, or in other ways, the forest types, standing volume, and rate of annual growth reflect the history of the particular area.

A forest of modest or larger size typically includes land of greatly differing productivity. Foresters have classified commercial forest sites according to their ability to grow wood annually, in fully stocked natural stands of the present forest types, with no intensive forestry, and during the most productive years of the growth cycle for trees of that forest type. The Forest Service uses five site productivity classes, ranging from Site Class 1, which can grow more than 165 cubic feet of timber per acre annually, down to Site Class V, which can grow between 20 and 50 cubic feet of wood per acre annually. Like the classification into commercial and noncommercial forests, the site classification is a physical-biological, not an economic, one.

Each of the four major ownership classes of forest exhibit great variation in site productivity (Table 3). Statistical data are not readily available to show the degree of variation within geographical areas smaller than states, but such data as there are and general knowledge agree that variation in site productivity often occurs within relatively small areas -- not only counties but often within single ownerships.[7] The sites of different productivity may be intermingled in a fashion comparable to the intermingling of farm land productivity classes as established by the Soil Conservation Service. Land slope, soil depth, site exposure (for example, north versus south slopes), and other factors often vary over relatively small distances.

7/ Clawson, ed., Forest Policy for the Future, pp. 142-145.

16

Table 3. Area and Productive Capacity, by Site Class, for Forests
of Different Ownership Classes, 1970

Area and productive capacity[a]	Approximate percentage in site class[b]				
	I	II	III	IV	V
National forests					
Area	3	10	20	38	29
Productive capacity	8	18	27	33	14
Other public forests					
Area	4	8	14	38	36
Productive capacity	11	16	19	36	18
Forest industry forests					
Area	6	12	28	37	17
Productive capacity	12	19	33	29	7
Other private forests					
Area	2	6	25	41	26
Productive capacity	4	12	34	37	13
All ownerships					
Area	3	8	23	39	27
Productive capacity	7	14	32	35	12

Source: Report of the President's Advisory Panel on Timber and the Environment, 1973, p. 35.

a/ Productive capacity was calculated by multiplying the midpoint of the class interval by respective acreage.

b/ Site classes I to V refer, respectively, to lands capable of producing growth of 165 plus, 120-165, 85-120, 50-85, and 20-50 cubic feet of timber per acre per year in fully stocked natural stands.

The national forests as a whole have an average productivity of 72 cubic feet of wood per acre annually, compared with 75 cubic feet for all forests and 88 cubic feet for forest industry forests. In the highly productive forests of the Douglas fir region of the Pacific Northwest, the national forests average 114 and the forest industry forests 145 cubic feet per acre annually. All of these physical differences in productivity understate the economic differences; many of the costs of timber growing are more related to area than to forest type, timber stand, or rate of growth. The forest industry lands are more productive on average than other ownership lands almost everywhere; the process of public land disposal was a selective one, and the timber operators sought and obtained the better forest lands. The national forests, on the other hand, because of their history, average lower in site class than many other forest ownership classes. But too much should not be made of this fact -- the national forests include a great acreage of highly productive forest land. If the dubiously commercial Site Class V lands are omitted, the difference among forest ownership classes is greatly narrowed, from 93 cubic feet per acre annual average on national forests to 98 on forest industry forests.[8]

Current Growth Compared with Productive Capacity

Vastly more important from an economic and policy viewpoint than the differences in biological capacity is the fact that actual net growth of wood in 1970 was only half of capacity of all forests, ranging from only 39 percent for national forests to 59 percent for forest industry forests.[9] The poor performance of the national forests is largely but not wholly due to the presence of the extensive stands of old growth timber on which little or no

---

[8] Clawson, Forests for Whom and for What?, p. 53. See also, Report of the President's Advisory Panel on Timber and the Environment, pp. 34-36.

[9] Ibid.

net growth (and sometimes even net loss) is taking place. Still worse, the
national forests in the Pacific Northwest show little upward trend in the
relation of actual to potential annual growth.[10]/

2. Use of the National Forests Today and in the Past

The Forest Service has always emphasized multiple use management of
the national forests. The agency's philosophy in this regard was given expression in the Multiple Use-Sustained Yield Act of 1960, which, in part,
expressed the objectives of national forest management as ". . . the management of all the variable renewable surface resources of the national forests
so that they are utilized in the combination that will best meet the needs of
the American people . . . harmonious and coordinated management of the various
resources, each with the other, without impairment of the productivity of the
land, with consideration being given to the relative values of the various
resources, and not necessarily the combination of uses that will give the
greatest dollar return or the greatest unit output." These somewhat imprecise and even somewhat contradictory instructions to the Forest Service may
be described as some, but not too much, economics.[11]/ The phrases "best meet
the needs" and "relative values" surely imply economic maximization, for it
is difficult to imagine a common unit of measurement for the various forest
outputs other than their economic value. "Not necessarily . . . the greatest
dollar return" might be interpreted as a repudiation of economic measures, or
it might be interpreted as a stricture to value those outputs not normally
sold for cash. As the national forests have actually been managed, economic

_10/ Marion Clawson and William F. Hyde, "Managing the Forests of the Coastal
Pacific Northwest for Maximum Social Returns," in a forthcoming volume report-
ing on a conference sponsored by the British Columbia Institute for Economic
Policy Planning, Vancouver, April 1974.

_11/ Marion Clawson, "How Much Economics in National Forest Management,"
Journal of Forestry, January 1974.

values seem to have been given little weight, as later parts of this report will show. Some foresters in the Forest Service, as well as some outside of it, actively reject economic values as guides to forest management.

The language of the Multiple Use Act surely poses severe problems for the Forest Service in implementation. In particular, over what unit of time and over what unit of area should multiple use be applied? If an attempt is made to apply it to every acre every year, the concept is impossible; if the application is over a considerable area of land and over a period of years, much more flexibility exists.[12/] The Forest Service has attempted its own resolution of the ambiguities of the Multiple-Use-Sustained Yield Act, by various studies and reports, whose length and variety preclude a full review here. One of the more ambitious and recent of these was its comprehensive ten-year plan, the Environmental Program for the Future (EPFF). However, many groups were not satisfied with the actual progress, though sometimes for different and even opposing reasons.

In the summer of 1974, the Forest and Rangeland Renewable Resources Planning Act (RPA) was enacted, which directed the Secretary of Agriculture to develop a long-range program for the nation's renewable resources. Throughout 1975, the Forest Service was working actively and hastily to meet the first deadline of the act, an assessment of the situation and a program, each due at the end of 1975. How far, or to what extent, this act will bring a greater measure of economic planning into the management of the national forests remains to be seen.

Use of National Forests Increased in the Past

Over the years all major uses of national forests except the grazing of domestic livestock have increased greatly (Table 4). In the approximately

12/ American Forestry Association, A Conservation Program for American Forestry, Washington, October 1975.

Table 4. Average Annual Harvest of National Forest Resources,
1925-29 and 1968-72

Resource	Annual average		1968-72 as multiple of 1925-29
	1925-29	1968-72	
Timber cut (billion board feet)	1.35	11.54	8.6
Recreation visits (millions)	6.3	188[a]	30
Wildlife (thous. big game killed by hunters)	216[b]	582	2.7
Water	n.a.	n.a.	probably 2.0[c]
Forage for domestic livestock (mill. animal unit months)	12.67[d]	8.60[e]	0.68

Sources: 1925-29: The Federal Lands Since 1956, pp. 58-60; 1968-72: Agricultural Statistics, 1974, pp. 550, 552, 554-555.

a/ Million visitor days, 1973.

b/ 1940-44 average.

c/ There is no data available on use of water flowing off national forests. With the volume of dam building, public and private, use in the latter period can hardly be less than double the former, even if total stream flow is unchanged.

d/ Figure is for 1929.

e/ Estimated from data on livestock numbers in Agricultural Statistics, 1974, p. 552, times average length of grazing session in 1964, as calculated from data in The Federal Lands Since 1956, p. 58.

forty-five years since the later 1920s (when some kinds of data first became available) until the period centering on 1970, the volume of timber harvested annually increased by more than eight times and the number of recreation visits (including visits to wilderness areas) increased by thirty times. Data on wildlife "harvest" or "production" are less satisfactory, but numbers of game animals killed annually nearly tripled from the early 1940s to the late 1960s. I estimate from various sources that, during the period from 1924 to the late 1960s, the amount of forage from national forests consumed by game animals, which provides a different measure of wildlife on national forests, rose by nearly seven times. Information on use of water flowing from national forests is still not satisfactory, but the amount of dam and other water developments on streams flowing at least in part from national forests suggests that use of such water must have doubled, even if total water volume remained unchanged.

Only in the case of domestic livestock grazing has there been a decrease in use of national forests; the decline of about a third from the late 1920s is on top of an earlier decline of about 60 percent from the peak in 1918. By the late 1960s, livestock grazing was down to 40 percent or less of its one-time peak, and was less than the grazing of wild animals.

All kinds of outputs from commercial forest land in the national forests rose over this period. Although the various uses of the national forests may, and sometimes do, impinge adversely upon each other at particular times and places, the forty-five-year record clearly demonstrates that each kind of use has increased substantially over time.

Prices and Unit Values of National Forest Products

Another measure of the value of national forest uses is provided by data on prices paid, or prices imputed, for the products obtained (Figure 1). The

Figure 1. Actual or Imputed Unit Prices (or Values) of
Stumpage, Grazing, and Outdoor Recreation
in National Forests, 1924-1972

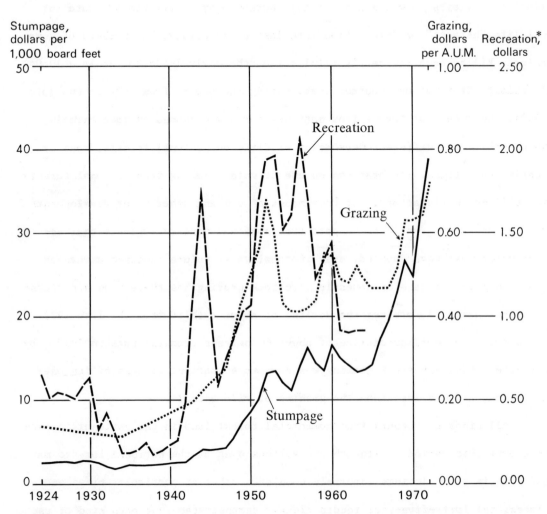

Stumpage, dollars per 1,000 board feet

Grazing, dollars per A.U.M.

Recreation,* dollars

*A value per recreation visit sufficient to make total calculated value of recreation equal to total value of timber sold.

price paid for stumpage (standing trees) sold from national forests fluctu-
ated between $2 and $3 per 1,000 board feet from 1924 to 1942; then ensued a
steep rise, only modestly variable from year to year, which carried average
stumpage value for all timber cut on national forests to nearly $40 in 1972;
prime logs, in good locations, brought prices from 2 to 5 times higher in
some sales. This apparent rise understates the true situation, however, for
the logs sold in recent years included many of grades and species and from
locations which would have been considered worthless at an earlier time.
Stumpage prices on all forests of all ownerships have risen greatly in recent
years, but more so on national forests than the average elsewhere, since the
national forests today often have better grade logs than do many other forests.

There is no comprehensive and generally accepted data series on the value
of outdoor recreation per unit (visit, or visitor day) from the national forests.
The actual price paid has been low, often zero, though rising considerably on
a relative scale in the past decade or more. Dividing the revenue received
from sale of timber by the reported number of recreation days gives a "recre-
ation-timber equivalency price" at which recreation total values would equal
timber sale receipts. This is purely a calculated number; it does not say
that recreation was sold at this price (it clearly was not) or that recreation
necessarily had this value. It simply says, given the volume of recreation
which did in fact take place on the national forests, at what "price" per unit
would the total revenues from recreation have equalled the total revenues from
timber sale. One may argue that recreation is more important than timber on
national forests, or that it is less important; this "price" does not consti-
tute evidence for either view but simply says this is an equivalency figure.

This "price" for outdoor recreation on national forests reflects several
factors: the volume of timber sold, the price per unit at which it is sold,

and the volume of recreation visits, among others. The "price" in the late
1920s was above 50 cents per visit; the volume and the price of timber sold
were both low but the number of recreation visits was proportionately even
lower. This "price" fell in the 1930s to around 20 cents per visit; both
volume and price of timber sold fell while numbers of recreation visits rose.
The "price" rose sharply during World War II as the volume and price of timber
rose modestly, while recreation visits were sharply curtailed because of travel
restrictions in those years. Following an immediate postwar adjustment, the
"price" rose during the 1950s to its highest levels, about $2 per visit; timber
volume and prices were soaring while numbers of outdoor recreation visits were
climbing more slowly. During the 1960s the "price" fell to slightly less than
$1 per visit as timber volume increased more slowly, timber prices stabilized,
and recreation visits mounted very rapidly. By the 1970s, as the price of
stumpage rose very sharply, the "price" of outdoor recreation also rose, in
spite of further increases in volume of outdoor recreation. If one were to
deflate these "prices" by some appropriate index of the general price level,
and were to smooth out the sharp fluctuations over short periods of time, very
little long-term trend would remain. The increased public demand for outdoor
recreation has taken the form of a greatly increased volume of this activity
in the national forests but the "price" trend is less clear.

One is at a loss to estimate "shadow prices" or "equivalency prices"
for wildlife and water; actual prices paid for these products from the
national forests are zero.

The fees paid for grazing of domestic livestock on national forests
have always been set by administrative action, not by marketplace bargaining.
There has been a long-continued political struggle over these fees, from about
1906 to the present, which it is unnecessary to relate here. For a considerable number of years the grazing fees were geared to the price of livestock

products, rising and falling proportionately to changes in those product prices, and ranged from 10 to 15 cents in the 1920s and 1930s to over 50 cents after 1950. A new formula for their determination is gradually raising average fees still further: to 72 cents in 1972 and still further in more recent years.

National Forests and Forest Industry Forests
Compared for Wood Production

The use and management of the national forests for wood production differs greatly from that of the forest industry forests (Table 5). Since the latter are owned and managed for business or profit reasons, one may reasonably assume that their management is, at least to a considerable degree, an economically rational one for the production and use of wood. While national forests have been established in permanent federal ownership for reasons other than profit (in the economic sense of that word), yet economic considerations and economic analysis can well be applied to their operations, especially for those products sold in the private market and generally competitive there with wood from private lands.

With an acreage of commercial forest only a third larger than forest industry forests, the national forests have three times the volume of standing sawtimber. No other major ownership class of forests has anything like as large an inventory of standing timber per acre as do the national forests. Although their total potential growth is greater than that for the forest industry forests, their actual net growth in 1970 was far less. In part this was due to the very high total mortality of timber on the national forests -- nearly three times, for sawtimber, that on the forest industry forests. Total removals, or harvest, in 1970 on national forests was low in relation to potential growth and in relation to volume of standing timber. The national forests were harvesting slightly more sawtimber than they were growing but were adding to their volume of growing stock.

Table 5. Comparison of Wood Production Indicators in National Forests
and Forest Industry Forests, 1970

Wood production indicator	National forests (92 million acres commercial forest)		Forest industry forests (67 million acres commercial forest)	
	Growing stock[a]/ (bill.ft.)	Sawtimber[b]/ (bill. board ft.)	Growing stock[a]/ (bill.ft.)	Sawtimber[b]/ (bill. board ft.)
Stand volume (inventory)	217.3	1,021.5	98.7	385.6
Potential annual growth[c]/	6.72	40.32	5.56	33.36
Net growth achieved in 1970	2.61	9.87	3.48	12.38
Mortality loss in 1970	1.34	6.30	0.68	2.37
Removals in 1970	2.18	13.17	3.67	18.22
Net change in inventory[d]/	+ 0.43	− 3.30	− 0.19	− 5.84

Source: The Outlook for Timber in the United States, Forest Resource Report
No. 20, Forest Service, U.S. Department of Agriculture, October
1973. Line 1, Appendix Tables 6 to 9, pp. 240-247; lines 3 and 5,
Appendix Table 21, pp. 273-275; line 4, Appendix Table 27, pp.
282-283; line 2, calculated from data in earlier tables in this
report.

a/ Net volume in cubic feet of growing stock trees 5.0 in diameter and over
at breast height, from a one-foot stump to a minimum 4.0 inch top diameter
outside bark of the central stem or to the point where the central stem
breaks into limbs.

b/ Sawtimber consists of logs meeting minimum regional standards of diameter,
length, and defect. Logs must be at least 8 feet long; softwood logs must
have a minimum diameter of 9.0 inches breast high (11.0 inches in California, Oregon, Washington, and coastal Alaska); hardwood trees must have
a minimum diameter breast high of 11.0 inches; minimum top diameter inside
bark must by 6.0 inches for softwood logs and 8.0 inches for hardwood logs.
International 1/4 inch log rule used. Volume of sawtimber realizable from
growing stock of sawtimber size depends on many factors; a rough overall
average is about 6 board feet per cubic foot (although theoretically a
cubic foot is 12 board feet).

c/ Potential growth per acre, by site class, from a fully stocked natural
stand with good but not intensive management, times total acreage in site
class.

d/ Net growth minus removals.

These comparisons of national forest and forest industry forest production of wood are more easily understood when put on a per-acre basis (Table 6). Gross wood growth per acre on national forests is 80 percent of that on forest industry forests, reflecting in part the somewhat lower biological productivity of the national forests and in part the relatively larger acreage of mature or old growth timber on them. But mortality per acre on national forests is almost double that on forest industry forests, reflecting almost entirely the greater age and maturity of the national forest timber. As a result, net growth per acre on national forests is not much above half that on forest industry forests.

All of these characteristics of wood growth and use in national forests merely reflect their large volume of old growth timber and the Forest Service commitment to slow conversion of such stands to managed rotations. The result is a large volume of standing timber, low annual net growth, much wastage of dead and dying timber, and a less than potential timber harvest.

In recent years harvest of softwood sawtimber from national forests has averaged about 30 percent of the total national supply. Lumber, plywood, pulp, and other forest products made from timber taken from national forests form part of the national supply of these products.

Everyone in the United States uses wood fiber in some form; it is almost impossible to imagine a life in the United States today without wood fiber -- a person would have to live in a cave, have stone furniture, pick up coal from the surface of the land, and find some substitute for toilet paper.[13/] To this extent, everyone is a beneficiary of wood production from national forests. This conclusion does not assert that national forests are efficiently managed for wood production nor does it assert that the wood produced from national

13/ Clawson, Forests for Whom and for What?, p. 1.

Table 6. Growth of Sawtimber Per Acre of Commercial
Forest in National Forests and Forest
Industry Forests, 1970

(board feet)

	National forests	Forest industry forests
Gross growth	176	220
Mortality loss	68	35
Net growth	107	185

Calculated from data in Table 5.

forests are their only benefits. Everyone in the United States helps to bear the costs of national forest management, including wood production in the form of taxes paid which form the basis for national forest appropriations.

Livestock Grazing on National Forest Land

The grazing of domestic livestock on national forest land occurs on nonforested parts, on noncommercial forest areas, and on forage growing in the relatively open commercial timber stands (such as ponderosa pine). The amount of forage secured from national forests is only a minor part of the total feed supply of the cattle, sheep, goats, and horses -- even for the West, the national forests provide less than 10 percent of their total feed supply. However, it is true that the national forests are seasonal (usually summer) ranges and often play a larger role in livestock production than their volume of feed alone would suggest.

To the extent that the meat produced by animals grazing on national forest land augments the total national meat supply, and hence helps to hold meat prices in check, everyone benefits from livestock grazing on national forest land. The ranchers whose livestock graze there benefit most directly, of course. As noted earlier, more of the total plant growth consumed by animals now goes to wild animals than to domestic livestock. The wild animals have important recreation values but their contribution to food supply, even in the West, is now small.

Outdoor Recreation in National Forests

The national forests are an important outdoor recreation area; in recent years the numbers of visits to national forests have about equalled the total number of people in the country. On the average, therefore, each person goes once per year to a national forest. This compares with approximately one visit a year to a unit of the national park system, twice a year to a federal reservoir, more than twice a year to a state park, and perhaps six times a year to a city or county park. However, like many averages, these can be misleading. For one thing, definitions of "visit" are not uniform from one organization to another, and some areas average more hours per visit than do others. In any case, a substantial proportion of the total public never goes to any federal or state area; perhaps no more than half of the entire population ever visits a national forest.

For all kinds of outdoor recreation areas, a distance-decay function is strongly operative; that is, the proportion of people visiting an area, and the frequency of their visits, declines rapidly as distance from the area increases. Most city parks draw their visitors from a radius of a very few miles, most all-day outing areas draw their visitors from less than 100 miles, and it seems probable that the overwhelming majority of the visitors to national forests live within 100 miles of the forest they visit. This is not to deny that some visitors travel much farther, or that visitors on long trips do not stay overnight in national forests, but it is clear that most visitors live closer. To a substantial extent, the national forests are a kind of super-state-park, larger, often less intensively developed, sometimes more scenic, but similarly located to most of their clientele. To this extent, the benefits of national forest outdoor recreation are more regional or local, and less national, than are the benefits of either their wood or their forage production, since the consumer products from the latter two outputs move nationally more than does the recreation output.

Wilderness on National Forests

"Wilderness" is a use or an attribute of national forests which has attracted much attention, and often much emotion, in recent years. It is difficult to describe, in part because of the lack of a wholly acceptable and unchanging definition of what constitutes a wilderness or a wilderness experience. When the Forest Service in the 1920s first established wilderness areas, by administrative declaration rather than by law, 100,000 acres was considered the minimum acceptable acreage for a wilderness area. Today, active consideration is given to a large number of roadless areas, each 5,000 acres or more, for possible inclusion in the national forest wilderness system. The Fish and Wildlife Service has proposed, and Congress has accepted, one wilderness area of only three acres; and private timber firms have been advertising land for sale, for private "wildernesses" of 20 acres or less. The minimum acreage one is prepared to accept for a wilderness area determines the number and acreage of potential wilderness areas within the national forests.

The early proponents of wilderness areas considered a complete absence of human activity (other than maps, trails, and portages) as a necessary characteristic of wilderness, and, indeed, the Wilderness Act of 1964 emphasizes the absence of human modification of the scene. But, in practice, many areas have been proposed for inclusion in the wilderness system whose virginity is more than in doubt, and proposals have been made for several eastern and southern wilderness areas which were logged long ago, sometimes had permanent settlements, but have since grown up again to forest.

The formally established wilderness areas of the national forests are one thing; their area and their use is known, at least approximately. The "de facto" or undesignated roadless areas that might be included in the

wilderness system are less clearly known. In July 1975, eighty-five areas
covering 11.6 million acres had formally been classified as wilderness within the national forests and another twenty-one areas containing 3.8 million
acres were included in proposals which had been submitted to Congress but
not approved on that date.[14/] In the early 1970s the Forest Service, acting
in part under the stimulus of some of the conservation organizations, reviewed the status and the suitability for wilderness of some 1,442 roadless
areas each containing 5,000 acres or more, which in total included over 55
million acres, of which about 18 million acres were commercial forest.[15/] However, many of these roadless areas were not suitable for wilderness classification, by standards in use until now. A strong supporter of wildernesses in
1971 estimated that only 20.9 million acres of national forests were suitable
for wilderness, on the basis of standards then in general use.[16/]

The roadless areas of 5,000 or more acres each within the national
forests have limited values for purposes other than wilderness. The very
fact that no public agency or private organization has thought it worthwhile
to build a road into them is substantial evidence of the values of other outputs -- if the values had been great enough, roads would have been built.
Most of these roadless areas have been open to mineral exploration and development since the earliest settlement days in their regions; while some valid
mining claims exist, the general absence of such claims suggests that mineral
values are not high. Most of these areas have been open to grazing by domestic

---

14/ Forest Service, draft report, "Assessment: The Nation's Resources,"
August 1975.

15/ President's Advisory Panel on Timber and the Environment, Report of the
President's Advisory Panel on Timber and the Environment, Washington, GPO,
April 1973.

16/ G. H. Stanley, "Myths in Wilderness Decision Making," Journal of Soil
and Water Conservation, 1971.

livestock, but the amount of such grazing has also been limited. Timber sales have not occurred in these roadless areas, in part because the costs of timber access roads would be high in relation to timber values. By and large, and with exceptions, the roadless areas are roadless simply because potential outputs other than wilderness are not large or are not valuable.

Because the wilderness areas of the national forests are more unusual than the more intensively developed recreation areas, they tend to draw some visitors from longer distances. However, the distance-decay function applies here also. To this extent, the benefits of wilderness are local or regional rather than national. The available data do not permit firm estimates but it seems likely that less than 2 percent of the total population visits a wilderness area in any one year and that less than 10 percent ever visits a wilderness area at any time during their lives. A good deal is made, by wilderness advocates, of the value of wilderness areas even to people who have never visited them and likely never will do so. It is argued that some people get great satisfaction simply from knowing that such areas exist. There is probably something to this argument, in the same way that everyone is richer because a national art museum exists even though one never visits it. The values of wilderness areas within national forests are spread more widely, in a geographic sense, than are the values of the more intensive recreation uses; but they are spread more narrowly, in terms of the numbers of people who gain some of these values.

3. What We Should Know, But Do Not Know Adequately,

About National Forests

It seems appropriate at this point to consider, very briefly, the kinds of knowledge the Forest Service, the Secretary of Agriculture, the Office of Management and Budget, the President, the Congress, the various industry and conservation groups who use the national forests, and the ordinary concerned citizen should have in order to reach reasoned decisions about the use and management of the national forests. The following four major kinds of information or knowledge are all essential:

1. The physical relation of output of every kind (wood, wilderness, recreation, water, and wildlife) to different amounts of each kind of inputs (management, labor, capital, management practices, user regulations, etc.), for each major site class on each national forest, under different forest management plans. The site classes should be defined in terms meaningful to the use; that is, site classification for wood growing is unlikely to be identical with site classification for wilderness, and so on for other uses. If certain amounts and kinds of fertilizer are applied to certain forest types, of certain site classifications, how much will wood growth be increased over what would otherwise occur and how long will that growth stimulation be manifest? Or if certain regulations as to spacing of wilderness parties are imposed and implemented, how many more wilderness users can enter a given area without decline in the quality of their wilderness experience? If timber harvest is planned on a forty-year rotation, how much different will be the outputs of all kinds and the inputs of all kinds, than if it is on a one-hundred-year rotation? These are but a few of scores of questions that might be posed. The Forest Service and others have answers, or at least rough estimates, for some of these relationships, at least for some areas, but accurate information is sadly lacking for the national forest system as a whole and such information as does exist is often not readily available to the citizen or the analyst who seeks it.

2. The degree to which one level of use or activity for one output of the forest interferes with or is compatible with a given level of use or

activity of another kind, also for the same relevant site classifications
mentioned above. It is obvious that some forest uses are incompatible with
others.17/ Preservation of an area for wilderness means that no timber
harvest can occur, for instance. Other pairs of uses may be made reasonably
compatible, as when timber harvest preserves watershed conditions. But such
general statements need quantification, as to actual trade-offs among pairs
of uses, refined for specific sites and locations, and modified to fit the
intensity of each use. With limited exceptions, these data are not available
for all relevant situations on national forests.

3. Shadow prices for an economic evaluation of services and commodities
not generally sold for cash, for locations with significant differences in
values. When, for any reason, valuable goods and/or services are provided at
administratively or arbitrarily established prices, rather than at prices
determined by buyers and sellers in the marketplace, economists have frequently
resorted to "shadow prices." These are the best estimates of what prices actually would be, had there been free trading in a reasonably competitive market
for the goods or services. Since shadow prices are necessarily estimates of
something that did not exist in fact, they are unavoidably somewhat imprecise
and often somewhat in dispute. Many conservationists and others have argued
that it is both impossible and undesirable to attempt to put monetary values
on such things as wildlife or wilderness. The answer is that it is unavoidable. Even the most dedicated wilderness buff, or one most vehement in his
denunciation of economics, will choose some alternatives as preferable to
others, when forced to choose -- some things are simply "not worth it." Difficult as is the economic valuation process and the estimation of shadow prices,

17/ Clawson, _Forests for Whom and for What?_, p. 40.

approximate as the results may be, and important as it is that economic
evaluations be leavened by judgments of informed and concerned people,
there is simply no alternative to making such estimates or not making them.
The alternatives lie with the care, skill, and explicitness of the value
estimates. The Forest Service research arm and some other researchers have
begun to make such evaluations but, generally speaking, such estimates are
inadequate in coverage and are not yet in use in the management of national
forests.

4. A capital account for national forests, based upon reasonable estimates of the present worth of the timber, land, and improvements, and upon
reasonable annual charges for use of this capital. A later section will show
that the value of national forests results in an annual capital charge which
greatly exceeds the direct annual management costs of the national forests.
Many foresters, especially foresters in public employment, seem to ignore
capital (interest) costs. There is good reason to believe that the national
forests are wasteful in the use of capital, but adequate data would measure
the extent of the wastage. Estimates of value of national forests should
include values for all outputs, not merely for wood production alone, and
should be made for significant site classes, as those suggested above.

If all the groups concerned with national forests had reasonably good
data on each of the above items, or even had the best explicit estimates for
each, for significant site classes, then decisions about use and management
of different parts of the national forest system could rest on a solid factual
foundation, in a way which is wholly impossible in their absence. Nevertheless, in spite of the data deficiencies, it is important to make the best
analyses one can possibly make today, both because decisions must be made and
should be as explicitly considered as possible, and because the best path

to better data is nearly always by the greatest possible use of existing data.

In emphasizing data deficiencies in this section, I do not mean to leave the impression that the Forest Service is unaware of these data needs or that it is not doing something about filling them. Some progress toward more accurate and more relevant data has been made in the past several years and more progress can be anticipated in the future. The Forest and Range-land Resources Planning Act of 1974 requires the Forest Service to make an assessment of the current forest situation in the United States and to pre-pare a national forestry program. The efforts of the agency and the comments of reviewers will almost surely point the way toward better data in the future. One can only hope that the rate of progress will be faster in the future than in the past, and that within a few years more precise analyses can be made than are possible today.

4. Potentials of the National Forests

What are the potentials of the national forest system to meet the needs or at least the economic demands of the American people for wood fiber in some form, for wilderness, for recreation, for water, and for wildlife?

Even if all the data one might want were available -- a most unlikely state of affairs ever -- there is still a problem of defining "potential." Two contrasting definitions help to point out the range of possibilities: (1) a biological potential for each use, assuming that use were the dominant one for all planning and management of the national forest system, with all other uses subordinate to this dominant one, and without regard to economic soundness or efficiency; and (2) a potential which has a presumption of rea-sonable economic efficiency, although (given the data deficiencies) not neces-sarily the economically most efficient one, and with considerable adjustment

of each use to others (although again, given the data deficiencies, not
necessarily the optimum such adjustment). "Potential" necessarily refers
to something not yet attained, and to something in the future rather than
in the present, hence estimates of potential at best can be only approximate,
but nevertheless may be very valuable.

By either standard of "potential," the national forest system can produce a good deal more of every good and service than it does today, without
serious environmental consequences and without damage to the productive potential of the national forests (Table 7).

Wood Growing Potential

In 1970 the national forests grew 2.6 billion cubic feet of wood, which
the Forest Service itself estimated was but 39 percent of the potential capacity of fully stocked natural stands at the active period of their growth
cycle.[18]

If all commercial forest acreage within the national forests were
managed on an intensive basis, with all other outputs of the forest subordinate to the one objective of producing wood and without regard to costs, I
estimate that 10.5 billion cubic feet of wood could be grown annually. This
increased output could be achieved only if all harvested areas were promptly
replanted within one year after harvest, rather than the much longer natural
regeneration time (averaging perhaps seven years); if seedlings were planted
at the optimum spacing to take full advantage of the sunlight, moisture, and
other natural conditions of each site, rather than the haphazard and often
very light restocking that usually occurs naturally; if stands were repeatedly
thinned to stimulate greater wood growth and to harvest stems that would

---

[18] Report of President's Advisory Panel, p. 36.

Table 7. Current and Potential Outputs of National Forests

Kind of output	Present output[a]	Potential output[b] Biological basis	Economic basis
Wood grown annually (billion feet^3)	2.6	10.5	6 to 7
Wilderness area[c] (million acres)	11.6	55	40
Outdoor recreation (million visitor days)	188	1,000	400
Water yield (volume)	Not measured	25% more	10% more
Wildlife, all kinds	Not measured	Many more	Slightly more

a/ 1970 for wood, some more recent year or average of years for others.

b/ Estimates of the author, see text for basis. For the biological basis, each use is considered dominant and other uses subordinate; there is no concern for economic efficiency. For the economic basis, each use is adjusted to other uses.

c/ Formally designated wilderness areas, excluding de facto wilderness. Assumes no major relaxation in definition of wilderness with regard to size of tracts or degree of nonwilderness use tolerated. Acreage measures, at best, opportunity for wilderness experience, not actual usage.

otherwise die and be unused; if stands were fertilized when growth response
would make such fertilization profitable; and if final harvest were complete --
clearcutting -- so that the cycle could start all over again.

National forest management to achieve the biological maximum wood production, without regard for other forest outputs, would nevertheless produce
a good deal of those other outputs. The land would still be a good watershed, there would still be much wildlife, and there could be a good deal of
outdoor recreation. If all the commercial forest were used for wood production, there would be no wilderness areas of commercial forest, although
there could be wilderness areas of noncommercial forest or of unforested
areas (some above timberline). This biological potential for wood growing
is meaningful only as suggesting, in necessarily approximate terms, where
the ceiling output may be -- a "ceiling" dependent upon our present knowledge
and imagination.

On the least productive national forest sites, intensive forestry would
generally not be economic.[19] Timber management could be concentrated on the
better sites, thus producing a great deal of wood, while at the same time
extensive areas could be set aside primarily for the production of other
forest outputs, including wilderness. As more consideration is given for
other products and services, including reservation of some wilderness areas
where timber could be grown economically, as well as many areas where such
growth would not be economic, and as consideration is given to the fact that,
for one reason or another, not all national forests would be producing at
their economic optimum, it still would be possible to grow 6 to 7 billion
cubic feet of wood annually. At the minimum, the national forests could
economically grow more than double their present annual wood growth.

_____

[19] Clawson, ed., Forest Policy for the Future, pp. 160-168.

Wilderness Potential

Any attempt to define potential wilderness encounters the definitional problem discussed previously. How large must each individual area be, and how much manmade disturbance is tolerable? Table 7 assumes basically the present concepts and definitions; any substantial further relaxing of standards for wilderness areas would change the possibilities. No attempt is made to estimate wilderness "output," which would include a measure of the amount of use but also, to be meaningful, should include some measure of the average "quality" of the experience -- a difficult, not to say slippery, task. Table 7 includes only acreage, not output. From the present approximately 12 million acres designated as wilderness, the total could rise to as much as 55 million acres (given present definitions), if no consideration were given to other uses and outputs from the national forests and without consideration of comparative economic or social values from wilderness as compared with alternative uses. Even at this biologically maximum acreage of wilderness, the output of other national forest products, including wood, would be high. Watershed, wildlife, and perhaps other values would be protected on the wilderness areas; on the areas biologically and psychologically unsuited for wilderness, these same outputs would be forthcoming and also more intensive outdoor recreation and wood production. The economic wood production potential of the national forests would be impaired only slightly by wilderness reservations, if present definitions are adhered to. The threat to wood output on the national forests, from the wilderness advocates, comes not so much from their demand for acreage to be reserved as wilderness as it does from their demands as to forest practices to be followed on the areas set aside for continued wood production.

When consideration is given to national forest outputs incompatible
with wilderness, the potential wilderness area is smaller, estimated in
Table 7 at 40 million acres. This would include all areas meeting present
wilderness standards of minimum acreage per area and of minimum human disturbance which had no commercial forest (some above treeline), or which had
commercial forest of Site Class V, and in addition a substantial acreage of
higher producing commercial forest. This might be less than the present
"de facto" wilderness area but it would be greatly above the presently
designated wilderness acreage. It should be noted that this is double what
Stankey estimated as the potential wilderness area in national forests.[20]
The 40 million acre estimate does not require a strict proof that somehow
wilderness is more "economically productive" than all other possible uses
of this national forest area; it simply says that there is a presumption
that an acreage of this magnitude, if the areas were carefully chosen, would
be "reasonably economic." Given the wood growing potential of the remaining
area under intensive forestry, this much acreage could be spared for wilderness if there were indeed an agreement to practice intensive forestry where
it was economic.

If the standards of wilderness definition are relaxed, there is almost
no limit to the area of wilderness within national forests, but large increases in area would be matched by substantial reductions in quality of
the wilderness experience. For instance, if areas as small as 20 acres (a
recent commercially advertised standard for wilderness) or even as large as
100 acres were to be accepted as "wilderness," then the potential acreage is
very large indeed. But such "mini-wildernesses" would surely not be free

20/ Stankey, "Myths in Wilderness Decision Making."

from evident effects of human use of adjoining areas, and thus the wilderness character of the present areas would be lost or at least severely compromised.

Outdoor Recreation Potential

When it comes to outdoor recreation other than wilderness, the seasonal recreation demands or desires of users, the location of national forests in relation to where users live, and the potential competition from other outdoor recreation areas such as state parks, all greatly affect the "potential." Even the estimate of biological potential includes some allowance for these factors; that is, if the American people lived in a different spatial pattern in the United States and sought to do nothing but enjoy outdoor recreation, several times as much use could be accommodated on the national forests. In fact, when greater consideration is given to these limiting factors, and when consideration is given to other uses of the national forests, their recreation potential is still double the present use. Under either of these potentials for outdoor recreation, there could be a large output of each of the other products or services of the national forests. There would be some adverse impacts upon wood production or at least upon wood harvest, and on some kinds of wildlife. Some of the development of moderately intensive outdoor recreation might be at the expense of wilderness, as some of the latter areas were invaded by roads and by visitors. But, on the whole, outdoor recreation could develop a long way in national forests without major impact upon most other outputs. Any loss of productive forest from wood production to recreation use, could be offset by more intensive forestry on those areas used for wood production.

Wildlife and Water Potential

Data are so poor for wildlife in national forests and for water yield from them that the potentials for these outputs must be stated in imprecise terms. Watershed research conducted by the Forest Service suggests that, if the national forests were operated to maximize water yield, without regard to other uses and without regard to costs involved, perhaps as much as 25 percent more water (in terms of stream flow) could be produced on their area. On many areas, trees and other deep-rooted vegetation would be replaced by shrubs and grasses, to provide cover to the surface of the soil but to reduce plant transpiration so that more water could reach the groundwater or subsurface flows. On other areas, trees might be cut in patterns that would facilitate snow accumulation in large drifts from which evaporation would be less than if the same snow were spread more evenly. Other practices might increase stream flows, but at costs. These increases in water yield could be obtained without lowering the quality of the water and without raising its temperature, although they would generally have some effect upon the seasonal distribution of flow. Even if watershed management were pushed to this biological extreme, without regard for costs and returns, there would still be a considerable volume of other forest outputs from the national forests. Wildlife and recreation might be adversely affected relatively little; wilderness and wood production might be affected more.

Introduction of other forest uses and a tempering by economic considerations leads me to a judgment of 10 percent more water. Similarly, if the national forests were operated primarily to maximize numbers and variety of wildlife, without regard for other uses and without regard for costs, then a lot more wildlife could be "produced." Even with modification to meet other uses and with some regard for costs, somewhat more wildlife could find a home in the national forests than do so today. These broad statements might need some modification when kinds of wildlife are concerned, for different species have different demands for habitat.

No specific timing is suggested for the achievement of the potentials. In the case of wood production, probably thirty years would be required, even if fully adequate efforts were directed to that end now -- the time required to convert the old growth stands that were scheduled for conversion is considerable, and some of the intensive forestry measures take time (genetic improvement, for instance), but often much less time than is ordinarily assumed. The wilderness area reservation could be made in a few years, if there were a consensus to do so. Other potentials would take intermediate time periods.

The potentials for each use, even with full allowance for accommodation to other uses and even with application of a substantial economic standard, are substantially above present outputs of the national forests. Some persons may object that it is impossible to increase the yield of everything -- that increases in one output must mean decreases in some other output. The most telling, if not logically the most defensible, argument is that this did not happen in the past. Table 4 presented data showing that essentially every forest use (excluding grazing of domestic animals) had increased greatly in the past. It may be argued that forty-five years ago there was great unused capacity in the national forests, which does not exist today. One major thesis of this report is that today there exists great unused productive capacity in the national forests, given today's technology and management possibilities.

The key to increased output of every forest good and service from
the national forests -- not merely wood, but all the others -- is intensive
forest management for wood production on some of the more productive forest
lands. This clearly produces more wood, and without serious impact on other
outputs even on the intensively managed areas. It also frees up a lot of
national forest land for the production of other outputs, including wilderness.

Some people are disturbed about the idea of intensive forest management. They equate it with "monoculture" and to them monoculture is Original
Sin. They conjure up ecological unbalances, biological deserts, and other
undesirable natural situations, and this leads them to oppose intensive
forestry. Literal monoculture, in which only one species of plant is
present over any area larger than a few square yards, is really very rare.
Even a wheat or corn field almost always has some weeds. In the American
forest scene, natural stands of mature Douglas fir or hemlock approach monoculture more closely than almost any other relatively natural forest situation. The dense tree stands effectively shut out sunlight on the ground
beneath them, and there is very little ground cover; and because there is
little or no food, there is very little ground-dwelling wildlife. Any
cutting, by any harvest method, opens up such stands, allows some sunlight
to reach the ground, and some new types of plants come in, and with them
some wildlife. Clearcutting of such stands results in an immediate blossom-
ing of other vegetation and often with an explosion of ground-living wildlife, such as deer. Birds and insects which live in the air but feed on
the trees are reduced by clearcutting, but those living on the ground are
increased.

The planting of a single tree species on a cutover area or on a bare former farm field rarely results in monoculture, at least not for some years and generally not at any time. Forest industry firms have planted pines on former farm fields in the South, but the national forests have included little of this because they consisted of other types of land. Even under these circumstances, Man may plant one species only, but other species of trees, shrubs, grasses, and annual weeds come in without his help and often over his strenuous efforts to keep them out. If the planted species is best adapted to the soil and climate, then it may be able to grow to the point where it crowds out its competitors. But this does not always happen and some of the unwanted species may survive until the next general harvest of the area. Timber harvest by any method, including clearcutting, is as likely to increase the number of plant and animal species present as it is to reduce the number.

There are, of course, some problems with single species forest tree management -- as there are problems with any species composition. Trees are subject to diseases and insects, and a single species puts all the risks on the one species. There may be fertility problems, and problems of "weeds," but, in all this, growing trees purposefully is not logically different than growing cultivated farm crops. Most of the fears grouped under the condemnations of monoculture simply have no basis in fact for intensively managed forests.

II. An Economic Perspective

5. Economics of National Forest Management

The national forests are a special kind of business enterprise. First of all, they are publicly, not privately, owned and managed. There are, of course, many other public business enterprises--TVA, the Bureau of Land Management, and others, which also produce large amounts of annual revenue. There are many special features of public business, wherein such enterprises differ from private ones. Secondly, related to but distinct from the foregoing, is the fact that profitmaking is not the primary motive in the management of the national forests. In fact, throughout their history the economics of national forest management have largely been ignored, and still are -- by the public, the Congress, the Executive Branch, and the Forest Service. One purpose of this section is to focus public attention on those ignored economics.

Some people might think that one distinguishing characteristic of national forests, as business enterprises, is that so much of their output is given away. Wilderness use, recreation, wildlife, watershed, and other uses pay little or nothing for their valued goods and services from the national forests. But this fact does not really distinguish national forests from most other forests. The forests owned by the forest industry and those owned by private individuals also provide most of these services, except reserved wilderness areas, sometimes to an extent per acre almost as great as for the national forests, and are also free or nearly so for these uses. The problem of the unrealized values from forest management is by no means confined to the publicly owned forests.

The sheer size of the national forests, whether measured in acreage or in annual receipts, and their potential for the future demand that they be considered as economic activities. They are simply too important for their costs and benefits to be ignored.

The Role of Prices in Any Society and in Any Economy

Prices of goods and services play several indispensable roles in any
society and in any economy, even in centrally planned and directed ones.
First, prices are a signal to producers, telling them how much to produce
and by what combination of inputs. Even when there are output targets, as
in a centrally planned society, the prices received for outputs go a long
way toward influencing producers, and actual output may reach planned output
only when prices are reasonably attractive to producers. In a freer economy,
where individual producers make their own decisions, prices of outputs and
of input factors are decisive, at least within rather wide limits.

Second, prices are a guide to consumers, helping them to decide how
much and what kinds of goods and services to consume, and how to allocate
their limited consumption income among various products and services. This
role is often pervasive when an attempt is made to establish prices by decree
or fiat; if the volume of goods available at the price does not equal the
volume consumers would choose at that price, then rationing of some form (maybe no more than extended queuing) is inevitable. Many Americans experienced
this form of rationing for gasoline in early 1974. In a free society, the
ability of consumers to choose, and the role of relative prices in guiding
those choices, are critical.

Third, prices are part of the income-allocative function, at least in
reasonably free societies and economies. When prices rise, producers gain
larger incomes, and consumers have suffered loss of real income, assuming
no offsetting other adjustments in either case. Questions may always be
raised as to what is "normal" or "fair," and both producers and consumers
may at times try to use political or other influence to change the terms of

trade in their favor. As long as bargains may be made as to quantities ex-
changed, then prices play a vital income-allocative role.

In a reasonably competitive market, both producers and consumers take
the market price as a "given" and adjust their production and consumption,
respectively, to that market price. When the market is significantly less
than competitive (in the economist's sense of that term), then each producer
or consumer must take into account the effect of his actions upon the market
price. If a producer bids up the price he is willing to pay for some input,
he faces the real prospect that his rivals will also bid up the price, and
neither may gain added supplies but each may have to pay more for the same
volume as previously. Similarly, if any producer lowers the price of his
output, his rivals may meet his prices and neither gains any added output
but each suffers a loss in income. Under these circumstances, both producers and consumers operate with one eye on their rivals, and every price
move is taken with consideration of probable competitor reaction.

When market prices are reasonably competitively determined (in the
above sense of the term), they measure opportunity costs to both producers
and consumers. That is, selecting one production model or one consumption
pattern over another requires giving up some alternative, and prices measure
the costs and values foregone. Under these circumstances, producers match
up their marginal costs with the market prices. That is, they expand
output until their marginal cost (including a "reasonable" or "normal" return on capital) just equals market price; many economists have shown that
this is their maximum profit scale of operation. When prices are affected
by the actions of the producer (or consumer) then he must take into account
the probable change in prices as a result of his decision, and now he matches

marginal value product against his marginal cost. If lowering prices a given percentage enables him to sell an equal percentage more output (elasticity of demand = 1.0), but his costs per unit of output remain unchanged (or even rise, if he is operating at a scale of diminishing returns), then his net income falls and the change in his prices would be a mistake.

All of this has direct application to national forests, if their management is to be economically efficient. The national forests are such a large percentage of the total supply of wood, recreation, wilderness, and every other output, nationally and more particularly in specific areas, that the actions of the Forest Service in large part make the market price. The Forest Service is required by law to sell timber at "competitive" sale, but in fact the competition is often less than perfect.[21] Even if there is spirited bidding for national forest timber, the very volume of timber offered for sale influences, if not dominates, the price of stumpage in that locality. The same is true of recreation and other outputs of national forests. It must be emphasized that the Forest Service cannot escape the responsibility of affecting prices of its outputs -- its very size inevitably results in its effect upon the market. This does not argue that the Forest Service has used its power wisely, or unwisely -- that is a separate matter, beyond the scope of this study.

The demand for the outputs of the national forests is probably inelastic, especially on a local or regional scale. There is an extensive body of economic theory which deals with the economically rational (i.e., profit-making) activities of firms which have monopolies or quasi-monopolies. One could

21/ Walter J. Mead, Competition and Oligopsony in the Douglas-Fir Lumber Industry, University of California Press, Los Angeles, 1966.

develop various economic models which would suggest under what circumstances the Forest Service could increase revenues from the national forests by exercising some part of its monopsony or oligopsony power, but these would be irrelevant because the national forests are not now operated, and almost surely never will be operated, to maximize profits arising from their economic power.

Leaving aside these possibilities for using monopoly power, the national forests could still be managed to increase their economic efficiency. This would require, among other things, the matching of the marginal cost of producing each output with prices obtained for it or with the estimated shadow price, for each national forest or local area, and for each site class of forest land. In such an analysis, values of all kinds of outputs should be included, not merely the value of the wood sold; and the costs of all inputs, especially on capital values, must be included. The relevant consideration is marginal cost, not average cost, and the price or value of outputs. If operating or investment capital is limited (as has generally been the case in the past), then the scale and form of operation should yield the same ratio of product value to marginal cost at all locations.

The full significance of these general economic principles when applied to national forests will become clearer in the following sections.

A Financial Balance Sheet for National Forests

Financial balance sheets have not generally been published for the national forests, but may be approximated (Table 8). This is a fairly conventional business balance sheet, somewhat abbreviated in order that it may all be gotten on one page.

Table 8. Financial Statement for National Forests, circa 1974

Account item	Total national forest system (mill. $)	Per acre of		
		Entire acreage ($)	Commercial forest acreage	
			Classes I - V ($)	Classes I - IV ($)
Capital structure:				
Value of standing timber[a/]	20,000	107	217	324
Value of forest land[b/]	20,000	107	217	324
Undepreciated value of manmade improvements[c/]	2,000	11	22	32
Total assets	42,000	224	456	680
Investment:[d/]				
in cash	196	1.05	2.13	3.08
in kind	120	0.64	1.30	1.94
Value of increased timber inventory, 1974 prices[e/]	42	0.22	0.46	0.68
Income:[f/]				
in cash	486	2.60	5.28	7.88
in kind	220	1.18	2.39	3.56
additional value of products and services provided at less than full market prices[g/]	490	2.62	5.32	7.93
Total annual output[h/]	1,238	6.63	13.45	20.05
Expenditures:				
in cash, all purposes	488	2.62	5.31	7.91
in kind[i/]	220	1.18	2.39	3.56
depreciation of manmade assets, 10%	200	1.07	2.17	3.24
payments to states & counties	79	0.42	0.86	1.28
interest on all assets, 5%	2,100	11.23	22.80	34.00
Total	3,087	16.51	33.53	49.99
Net annual income, cash & noncash	(1,849)	(9.87)	(20.08)	(29.94)

a/ The Outlook for Timber in the United States shows a 1970 inventory of
1,021 billion board feet of sawtimber on national forests. On the
basis of $40 per 1,000 board feet, which is an approximate recent
average for timber sold from national forests, the value of the standing sawtimber (ignoring values for growing stock of less than sawtimber
size) would be slightly in excess of $40 billion. This value has been
cut in half, to reflect a reasonably early (10 to 20 year) liquidation
value.

b/ Excludes timber values; averages about $110 per acre for all national
forest land; also assumes reasonably early liquidation value.

c/ The Federal Lands Since 1956, p. 54, report $1,160 million in 1963;
estimated to have risen to $2,000 million by 1974.

d/ Investment in cash data from Forest Service (personal letter July 17,
1975 from John R. McGuire, with enclosures); roads, trails, other construction, and purchase of land.
Investment in kind is road building allowance in timber sales contracts;
12 billion board feet, assumed $10 per 1,000 board feet road building
allowance in sale price.

e/ The Outlook for Timber in the United States shows that in 1970 harvest
slightly exceeded growth of growing stock for softwoods but that growth
exceeded harvest by about 450 million cubic feet for hardwood growing
stock. Converted to board feet, 6 board feet per cubic foot; $80 per
1,000 board feet for softwood, $30 per 1,000 for hardwood.

f/ Income in cash includes receipts from mineral leases on national forest
lands acquired by purchase from private owners; excludes them from national
forest lands reserved from public domain. Income in kind includes all of
road building allowance plus $100 million in working funds, cooperative
agreements, etc., where the national forest user agrees or is required as
a condition of timber harvest or other use to undertake certain restoration
or other activities.

g/ Estimated on basis of 170 million recreation visits other than wilderness
at an average value of $2 each, 10 million wilderness area visits at an
average value of $10 each, and water supply at $50 million. Wildlife
values assumed included in recreation and wilderness values. States may
benefit from wildlife values, for instance in sale of hunting licenses.
No allowance is made for the possibility wood and forage are sold at less
than a full value.

h/ Increased timber inventory, cash and kind receipts, and values of products
not sold for cash.

i/ These are the same items described in f/; they appear both as income and
as outlay.

The most difficult, and the most neglected, aspect of a financial balance sheet for the national forests is the capital account. There are no official estimates of the reasonable present value of the national forests. Acquisition costs are irrelevant to present and future management decisions on the national forests. The desired figure is a reasonable estimate of the present value. For reasons which should become clearer in following pages, capitalization of earning power is not a reasonable approach to present value. A sale or liquidation value, as best this can be estimated, gives an alternative use or alternative value approach to present value of the national forests, and has been used here.

In 1970 the national forests contained slightly in excess of 1,000 billion board feet of standing sawtimber. Recent prices of stumpage sold from national forests have averaged close to $40 per 1,000 board feet and prices for the next decade or two are likely to be higher. This might suggest that the value of the standing sawtimber was $40 billion; for reasons outlined below, this is too high. But it should be noted that there is a volume of growing stock, in addition to the sawtimber, with perhaps as much as one-fourth the volume of wood as in the sawtimber. Growing stock includes trees above 5 inches in diameter, but not yet of sawtimber size (11 inches diameter along the Pacific Coast, 9 inches elsewhere). There is a considerable volume of wood, and much future growing stock, in trees of less than 5 inches diameter, ranging downward to small seedlings just planted.

The present sawtimber volume could not be liquidated by sale and manufacture into lumber, plywood, or other products in ten years, or even in twenty years probably, even if it were desired to do so --

processing capacity is too limited, markets are too restricted. It would,
of course, be possible to sell the standing timber (and the land) to private
owners who would liquidate the timber over a longer period. It would not be
difficult to construct various economic models, with varying rates of liquidation of the timber, and various discount rates to arrive at a present worth
of the timber. These models would necessarily rest upon rather arbitrary
assumptions; instead, Table 8 simply uses half of the apparent value of the
sawtimber, with nothing included for the trees of smaller size, to arrive at
a present value of timber of $20 billion.

The land in the national forests, without regard to the present stands
of trees, has also been estimated to have a present value of $20 billion. It
is assumed that the land could be auctioned off to persons or groups who wanted
recreation property, including "wildernesses" of their own, to firms or persons
who wanted to grow timber, to ranchers for grazing, and to other types of owners.
Sales of private land in regions where the larger national forest acreages lie
suggest that this is a reasonable figure.

In addition, the capital account includes $2 billion for the undepreci-
ated present value of roads, trails, and other permanent improvements on the
national forest. Combined, these estimates of the components of value come
to $42 billion as the reasonable present value of the national forests. In
a later section, the significance of this figure, of the appropriate interest
rate, and of the use of alternative investment figures will be explored in
more detail.

Every natural resource which is worth using yields some surplus of
returns above costs, a surplus which the economist calls "rent." This arises
even when no contractual rent is paid by the user to any owner -- it can be

internal to the operations of the owner-user firm or person. The willingness of buyers to pay for natural resources is based upon their estimates of probable "rent." They may include psychic values in estimating income and rent, as when a family owns a beautiful home to which it is attached, or an urban businessman owns a ranch because he likes ranch life, or when someone owns a tract of forest land for personal reasons.

If our estimate of the value of the national forests is approximately correct, it means that, in total, private buyers would calculate a rent, including psychic or noncash values, high enough to justify an investment of $42 billion. In thus estimating the sale or liquidation value of the national forests, there is no suggestion that they actually be sold or transferred from public to private ownership. In the United States today, such an action is socially and politically unthinkable. Since we do not propose to sell the national forests, this method of determining their value cannot be put to the test, but this does not in the least invalidate the calculation of such value nor the use of rent based upon it as a factor in economic management of the national forests. If this is a private value, based upon a privately estimated rent, should the public enterprise do any less than earn the same rent, when all noncash as well as cash values are figured in? What justification is there for tying up very large sums of public capital in a publicly owned natural resource unless the social product from the management of that capital equals or exceeds the private rent from use of the same resource? This, in essence, is the challenge to national forest management today.

Rent, in this sense of the term, from the management of the national forests should be maximized when all products are included at their actual or shadow prices, whichever is higher. This requires the calculation of capital values and capital charges. When rent, so defined, is maximized, so is social product maximized, for costs of producing outputs have been deducted. It is not necessary that rent actually be paid to anyone in order that its calculation and maximization be a useful management process. As long as there are different methods of operating the national forests, some of which will yield more imputed rent than others, then the inclusion of rent from the next most profitable form of use is a proper charge against operations in any specific way. It is possible to choose that method of operation which maximizes rent, so defined, and with all outputs valued at their full value. The methods of managing the national forests are many and varied and so are the amounts of capital and hence the appropriate capital charges.

In recent years, the Forest Service has been investing between $100 and $200 million of appropriated funds each year, chiefly for roads and trails but also for land acquisition. In addition, buyers of timber and some other users of national forests have been required to construct roads or make other improvements as part of the arrangements whereby they secured national forest products or services. The sale price of timber includes an allowance for road construction; although the timber buyer constructs the road, he is paid for it by some of the timber he gets from the forest. The road investment of this kind has been estimated at $100 million annual average in recent years; since the same figure enters both the income and the expense account, as will be shown later, the precise figure does not affect the net financial balance.

In 1970, the latest year for which data are available, the national forests were adding to their volume of standing timber, a slight reduction in softwood growing stock (mostly in the West) more than offset by a considerable net addition to the volume of hardwood growing stock (primarily in the East and South). The estimated value of this increased inventory (see note e to Table 8) is conservative and may understate the added value. It makes no allowance for the rising value of timber; if this were included, the vast inventory of timber in the national forests would show a substantial capital gain, perhaps not every year but over a period of years.

The cash income from the national forests in fiscal 1973-74 (reported in Table 8) was almost $500 million, and over 94 percent of this was from timber sales. The grazing receipts mostly came from the nonforested parts of the national forests, as did some of the receipts from recreation and other miscellaneous sources. If these are eliminated, the cash receipts from the forested parts of the national forests are almost wholly from timber sales. The figures shown in Table 8 are receipts actually obtained; some may argue that the products or services sold for cash were sold at less than their full market value.

Many services from national forests are available to the consumers of such services at prices which do not reflect their true value, and a financial statement must include some allowance for these values. Wilderness use, recreation use, wildlife, and water from the national forests all have values far in excess of the zero amount paid for them. Until such services are actually sold or charged for, any estimate of their value is unavoidably approximate. In the estimated values in Table 8, no allowance is made for the effect charges would have on the volume of use; that is, estimated rates per unit of use are applied to the present volume of use, which is not discounted for the effect a price would have on volume. It is extremely difficult to put reasonable values on these uses. The groups gaining them emphasize their value but they do not acknowledge their obligation to pay; in this, they are caught in a dilemma. If the values are high, the lack of payment is more inequitable, while if the values are low

the argument for protecting these values is weakened. The values in Table 8

may be too generous, but at a minimum the values are considerable.

Some of the management expenditures in the operation of the national

forests are cash outlays, paid out of appropriated funds. In Table 8, cash

outlays almost exactly equalled cash receipts. Almost exactly half of the

cash outlays were for "national forest protection and management," more than

a fifth were for forest fire fighting, and the rest for miscellaneous other

purposes, including disease and insect control and brush disposal after timber

sale. It is very difficult to compare sources of receipts and purposes of

expenditures.[22/] In fiscal 1972, $40 million was appropriated expressly for

recreation (presumably including wilderness) while receipts were less than

$8 million; for wildlife, the figures were $6 million and zero, respectively;

and for water, $13 million and less than half a million, respectively. Timber

management, in contrast, had $96 million appropriated and $321 million in

receipts. However, substantial other costs in the national forests, such as

road building, fire control, and insect and disease control, have values for

all outputs of the forest, and it is not easy to allocate their costs against

any particular output. Based upon comparative receipts, timber management

gets less than its share of the management outlays; based upon the Forest

Service's estimates of needs, the nonpaying uses of the forest get less

management expenditures than are justified.

The income in kind is equal to the expenditures in kind. To the ex-

tent that one is overestimated or underestimated, so is the other, and the

---

22/ Clawson, Forests for Whom and for What?, pp. 141-144.

64

net balance is not affected. The depreciation of investment in past manmade improvements is an important item of cost. Under law, a share of the
national forest receipts are paid to the states and counties in lieu of
taxes. At this time, no judgment is expressed as to whether the level of
such payments is reasonable, too low, or too high; paying a share of
receipts is an undesirable way to recognize the legitimate claims of state
and local government.[23/]

The dominant cost in Table 8, more than two-thirds of the total, for
national forest management is the interest charge on the investment. The
annual cost in the table rests on the current value figure, whose origin
was discussed earlier, and upon a 5 percent annual interest rate. Since
the valuation figure is unavoidably approximate, question may well be
raised as to the accuracy of the analysis based upon it. Two major further
points can be made, to put this figure and the whole issue in perspective.
First, a 5 percent interest rate is too low for today and for the foreseeable future; 7-1/2 percent would be more reasonable today, and this adds
50 percent to the annual capital charge. Second, suppose that the present
value is only half of that shown in the table: no major conclusion of this
analysis is changed thereby! If the present value were only half as large
and if the interest rate remains at 5 percent, then the annual capital charge
is still by far the greatest single cost -- only half instead of two-thirds
of the total, but still far larger than anything else; and the rate of return
on present value is less than 1-1/2 percent instead of about 1/2 percent --
better, but still not good. If one accepts the value figure of Table 8 and

23/ Clawson and Held, The Federal Lands: Their Use and Management, pp.
313-330.

uses a 5 percent interest rate, the national forests incur a deficit of nearly
$2 billion annually, or about $9 per capita of the whole population.

By any reasonable estimate, the annual interest cost of national forest
management is very high. The national forests, which in the popular mind are
the embodiment of wild and rustic values, are in fact a highly capital-using
enterprise, at least as now managed.

Before we attempt an explanation of this economically poor record and
before we suggest how it might be improved, it is essential to examine some
other aspects of the income and expenditure patterns of national forests, and
this is done in the sections which follow.

Regional Pattern of National Forest Expenditures

The previously outlined relationship of marginal costs to prices or
estimated shadow prices of each output should apply to each region of the
Forest Service. The values of all outputs, including those sold for cash
and those made available at nominal or zero charges, and including changes
in inventory, should be calculated. Likewise, the full costs, including
those in kind and including charges on capital values, should also be calculated and marginal costs estimated. If all values are included and are
accurately estimated, there is little social justification for expenditures
which exceed them. If rents sufficient to justify the capital values can
be earned by private operation, there is little justification for public
operation which earns any less. The fact that alternative methods of
national forest operation exist, by which different amounts of rent can be
earned, mean that the rent-maximization test can be applied even though the
lands are in public ownership and will remain so. Costs should not ignore
capital charges, for these, though unpaid in cash, are generally greater

than all other costs combined. If funds available to the Forest Service did not permit a scale and a method of operation such that marginal values only barely exceeded marginal costs, then optimum economic management requires that operations in each region should be at a scale and in a method which preserves approximately the same relationship between marginal costs and values in all regions.

In fact, data are not available, or at least not readily available to one outside the Forest Service, to make this type of comprehensive analysis. Data are available on cash receipts and cash expenditures by regions. There are good reasons to judge that the relationship between all costs and all values would not differ greatly from the relationship between cash costs and cash values. That is, where cash values are high, noncash values may be high also. For instance, California as a Forest Service region has relatively high cash receipts in relation to cash costs; it is probable that complete and accurate data would show that the value of outdoor recreation, wilderness, water, and wildlife is relatively high in California also. Likewise, where cash costs are high, noncash costs (including interest, but also road costs paid for by timber) may also be high. One can imagine circumstances where total values would diverge more than proportionately from cash values -- especially valuable recreation or wilderness values, as well as large changes in inventory, or others; but these are less likely to arise on a regional than on a local basis. Likewise the relationship between total values and total costs may be a reasonable indication of the relationship between marginal values and marginal costs.

The regional pattern of expenditures of operating and investment funds available to the Forest Service during the five most recent years for which

data are available has been economically wasteful (figures 2 and 3). Except
for Alaska (where expenditures are lower), a Forest Service region seems to
require $20 to $30 million dollars cash management expenditures even when
cash receipts are under $10 million; and expenditures do not begin to rise
proportionately after revenues pass a level of about $40 million per region.
The shortfall in management expenditures, in relation to revenue, is considerable for the California region of the Forest Service and is especially
marked for the Pacific Northwest region. The relationship for investment
expenditures is similar but more marked; investments rise relatively little,
no matter how much receipts rise. It may be objected that natural conditions
in the different Forest Service regions are different and that both operating
and investment expenditures must be higher in some regions than in others.
Conceivably, some of the scatter in points on the charts would be reduced,
were the comparisons reduced to a per acre basis and were allowance made for
values of forest outputs not sold for cash, but it is extremely doubtful that
the basic picture of these two figures would be changed thereby.

The data in figures 2 and 3 do not touch upon the issue of how wisely
and/or efficiently expenditures are made in any region. To some extent, that
question is taken up in the sections which follow. Neither do these figures
assert that spending more money in the regions where it appears too little
is now spent would necessarily be wise -- the added expenditures might be
for unwise purposes, or on the wrong sites, or for the wrong management techniques. Neither do they say that cutting back expenditures in the relatively
high expenditure regions would necessarily be wise -- the cut-backs might be
in the wrong activities, for the wrong practices, or in the wrong locations.
The two figures do raise many questions, which it should be useful to explore
further.

Figure 2.   Cash Management Expenditures and Cash Receipts, by

National Forest Regions, Fiscal 1970-1974

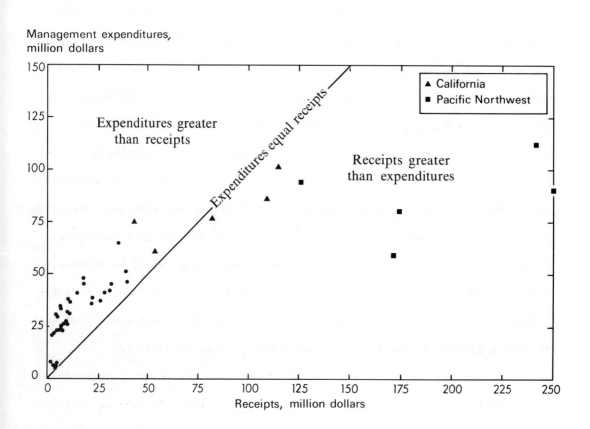

Figure 3. Cash Investment Expenditures and Cash Receipts, by
National Forest Regions, Fiscal 1970-1974

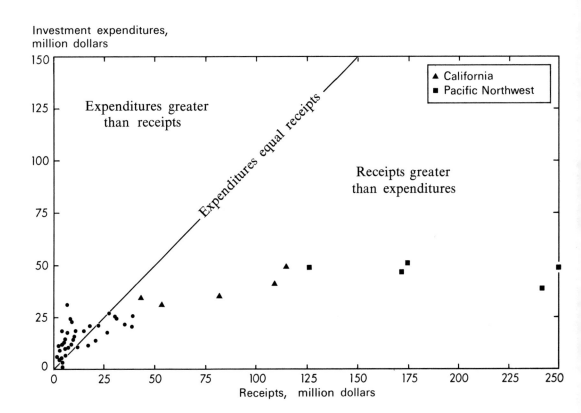

The regional average cost per 1,000 board feet for timber management, reforestation, and timber stand improvement may be compared with the regional average value per 1,000 board feet of timber sold (not necessarily harvested in that year) for two years (Figure 4).[24] In fiscal 1972, stumpage prices were comparatively low, while in fiscal 1973, under the impetus of a very active housing market and of Japanese purchases of logs in this country, stumpage prices were much higher. On the chart, the prices received are net of the 25 percent payments made to the counties in which the national forests lie, and the cost figures are exclusive of the Knutson-Vandenburg funds which timber purchasers contribute for restoration of harvest sites. The chart shows purely cash expenditures from appropriated funds as compared with net cash receipts.

In each year there was a significant though not high negative correlation between cost and value per 1,000 board feet. In 1973, when stumpage prices were high, only the Northeast region (9) and Alaska (10) had costs higher than price, but in 1972 both those regions and the Rocky Mountain region (2) had such an unfavorable relationship. In 1973, in those regions where stumpage values were about $50 per 1,000 board feet, these costs averaged about $10 per 1,000 board feet; in those regions where stumpage values were less than $20 per 1,000 board feet, these costs were $15. In 1972, the relationship was even more marked and less favorable. Where timber values per unit of volume are low, management costs per unit of volume are high, and vice versa.

In making this comparison, it should be emphasized that the costs in Figure 4 are not total costs, not even total cash costs of national forest management, for they make no allowance for a proportionate share of fire

---

24/ I am indebted to Lawrence W. Libby who dug these data out of Forest Service records and made them available to me.

fighting, road construction, and other costs that are of benefit to all outputs of the forest. They relate to those costs directly chargeable to timber management.

The regional comparison can be approached in another way (Figure 5). The least costly region (Pacific Northwest), in terms of these costs per 1,000 board feet, produced about 4 1/2 billion board feet of timber sales in 1972. At each successive increment of timber, in other regions, costs per 1,000 board feet rose. The total spread is from slightly less than $5 per 1,000 board feet to somewhat more than $15. Only three regions -- the larger ones -- had costs below average, while six regions had costs above average. Nearly 80 percent of the total volume of sales that year were at costs only slightly above average or less; the smaller high-cost timber produced a relatively small share of total national forest sales that year.

Comparisons by Separate National Forests

A closely similar situation is revealed when total expenditures are contrasted with total receipts, for all the individual forests (Figure 6). It seems to cost from $1 to $3.5 million to operate a national forest even when cash receipts are less than $1/4 million; cash outlays rise more or less proportionately to cash receipts up to a level of perhaps $2.5 million receipts, after which there is very little relationship between receipts and expenditures -- although a few forests with high receipts also have high expenditures, some forests with high receipts have only average expenditures. By far the greater proportion of the national forests incurred a cash deficit in 1972. It is, of course, possible that a complete accounting of all values produced by national forests would change this picture; it surely would increase the level of income. But a full accounting of all costs would also raise the level

72

Figure 4. Cash Cost of Timber Management, Reforestation, and Timber

Stand Improvement in Relation to the Value of Timber

Sold, by National Forest Regions, 1972 and 1973

NOTE: The numbers refer to national forest regions, according to the U.S.

Forest Service designations 1 = Northern; 2 = Rocky Mountains; 3 = Southwest;

4 = Intermountain; 5 = California; 6 = Pacific Northwest; 8 = Southeast; 9 =

Northeast; and 10 = Alaska. The region previously designated as 7 was

combined with region 8.

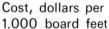

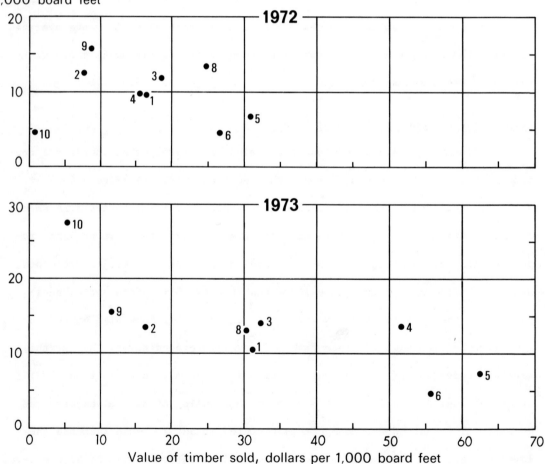

Figure 5. Volume of Timber Sold (Cumulative by Regions) at

Specified Costs Per 1,000 Board Feet, 1972

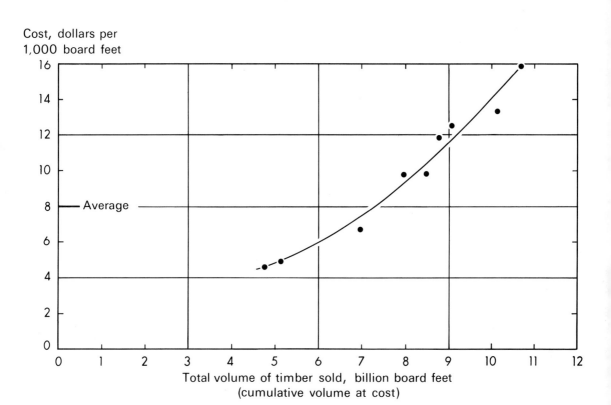

Figure 6. Total Cash Expenditures and Total Cash Receipts, by

National Forests, Fiscal Year 1972

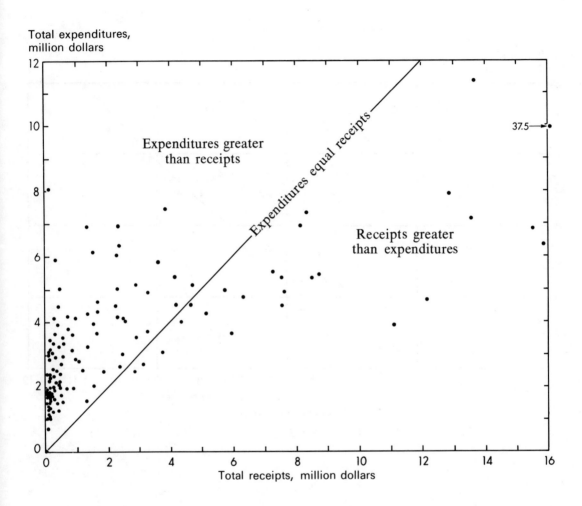

of costs substantially. While some individual national forests might have their relative positions shifted, it is by no means clear that the general picture would be changed by a more nearly complete accounting.

The differences among national forests can be approached in another way, by building up a composite or average picture of a national forest in the Southwest region and comparing it with one in the Pacific Northwest (Table 9). The average Southwest region national forest has a smaller commercial forest acreage, much less allowable cut, and cash revenues less than one-tenth those of the average Pacific Northwest forest, but its expenditures were 60 percent as high in 1972. It is probable that grazing was more important in the Southwest, but one would be hard pressed to assert that the noncash values were greater there. On the Southwest region forest, actually _more_ is spent per acre of commercial forest; even if corrected for the other outputs and the areas of national forest lacking commercial forest, it would appear that as much per acre is spent on the relatively unproductive forests of the Southwest as is spent per acre on the more productive national forests of the Pacific Northwest. The number of employees in relation to area is about the same and the annual cost per employee is actually higher in the Southwest. In the Southwest there are fewer timber access roads in relation to forested area but vastly more in proportion to the volume of timber sold. This latter relationship is in part a reflection of the typically lower volume of timber per acre in the Southwest; a road to open up an area will tap a smaller volume of timber in the Southwest.

Although none of these data are perfect for our purposes, they strongly suggest that the geographical pattern of expenditures on national forests is economically unsound and wasteful.

Why should this be so? A fuller explanation is given in a later section, but a few comments might well be made here. First of all, it is not clear how

76

Table 9. Comparisons of National Forests in Southwest
and Pacific Northwest Regions, Fiscal Year 1972

Item	Average of 13 national forests in Southwest region	Average of 19 national forests in Pacific Northwest region
Area of commercial forest (1,000 acres)	442	862
Allowable cut, sawtimber (mill. bd. ft.)	35	231
other products (1,000 cords)	29	neg.
Actual cut, sawtimber (mill. bd. ft.)	28	256
other products (1,000 cords)	8	neg.
Forest receipts per forest (thousand dollars)		
forest products	656	8,629
total	823	8,695
Forest expenditures per forest (thousand dollars)	3,528	6,011
Total receipts per acre of commercial forest (dollars)	1.86	10.09
Total expenditures per acre of commercial forest (dollars)	7.98	6.97
Ratio, total receipts to total expenditures	0.23	1.45
Employees per forest[a/]		
permanent	130	276
temporary	86	139
Employees per 1,000 acres of commercial forest[a/]		
permanent	0.294	0.320
temporary	0.195	0.161
Total receipts per employee (dollars)	3,810	20,952
Total expenditures per employee (dollars)	16,333	14,484
Timber access roads per forest (miles)	384	1,698
per 1,000 acre commercial forest	0.87	1.97
per million dollars of timber receipts	591	197

Source: U.S. Forest Service reports of operations by individual national
forests, published by National Forest Products Association.

neg. = negligible.

a/ Including a proportionate share of regional office employees.

far the decision to spend appropriated funds in the regional and functional patterns described here was made by the Forest Service and how far those decisions were imposed upon it by other parts of the Executive Branch or by the Congress. A common popular explanation of a seemingly uneconomic governmental action is "politics," meaning that some interest group had been able to influence or determine governmental action to its particular advantage. There may indeed be "politics" behind the geographical allocation of national forest expenditures, but this is not readily apparent in the public record, such as the debates and hearings on appropriation bills. Intuitively, one suspects that other forces are dominant. The later sections of this report will attempt to explain which ones.

Expenditures and Income by Site Class

The foregoing analysis does not directly deal with the matter of expenditures and income by productivity site classes. The data are lacking to do this. Indeed, it would be hard to assemble such data, unless field records were kept on this basis. Tracts of national forest of different productivity classes are intermingled, and boundaries are not always apparent on the ground. Many costs are "overhead" in the sense that they are a total for the national forest or at least for the ranger district, and their allocation to activities and to land of different site characteristics would often be difficult. Such analyses, if they could be made, would be extremely important. Some rather general studies made at Resources for the Future strongly suggest that, in terms of economics, timber production is vastly more favorable on the highly productive than on the less productive sites, and that timber growing on Site Class V is dubiously economic at best.[25]

---

[25] Clawson, Forest Policy for the Future; and Clawson and Hyde, "Managing the Forests."

It is highly probable that operating and investment expenditures are unwisely distributed among forest land of different site qualities. The pattern
of expenditures by regions and by forests strongly suggests that too much money
is being spent on poor sites and not enough on good ones. The available data
suggest that this is true within regions where favorable receipt-expenditure
ratios exist as well as in regions where the ratio is less favorable.

The Forest Service site classification is a biological, not an economic
one, as we have noted previously. It is based on fully stocked natural stands
and on a system of forest management which might be described as good natural
stand management. A site classification appropriate for management decisions
should be an economic one, and it should include information on the response of
different sites to more intensive management. It would not be easy to develop
such an economic site classification, and it would change as economic conditions
changed, at least if changes in the latter were large. Consideration would have
to be given to such factors as the value of the wood per cubic foot, to the
effects of slope and topography upon road and other harvest costs, to location
of the site with respect to major transportation arteries and to markets. While
it would be difficult to develop a complete and wholly satisfactory economic site
classification system, reasonably good judgments of men experienced in timber
management and harvest would be infinitely preferable to management and investment schemes which gave little or no recognition to site characteristics. As
it is, many incidents about national forest management are reported which suggest
strongly that differences in productive capacity are not given much weight in
actual management and investment decisions.

While the differences in site quality are best understood and better defined for wood growing than for any of the other outputs of national forests,
the same general idea is applicable to all other outputs also. Some sites are

better for outdoor recreation than are others, some will produce more and more
varied wildlife than others, some have higher watershed values, and so on, for
all outputs of the forest. Difficult as it may be to define site grades and
characteristics accurately for these other outputs, yet the best available
judgment is likely to be far more efficient than neglecting or ignoring the
variations in site productivity.

Finally, it must be emphasized that the economic difference between a
good site and a poor one is much greater than the physical differences between
them. Timber management may be as expensive on poor sites as on good ones --
Figure 4 indeed suggests that costs are likely to be higher on poor than on good
sites. There is an old saying in the timber industry that costs are incurred
per acre while income is secured per unit of wood grown and sold. If physical
output per acre is double on one site as compared with another, and if management costs are fairly high in relation to income, then net income on which economic value must rest may be ten times higher on the more than on the less productive site.

Capital Use and Waste in National Forests

Operation and management of all forests, whether publicly or privately
owned, involve large amounts of capital in land, standing timber, improvements,
such as roads, and necessary machinery. Timber is an unusual form of capital,
for the same tree may be either capital or output. If cut, it is output; if
allowed to stand and grow, it is capital. Once a tree gets large enough to
produce a merchantable log for pulp or for lumber, it can be harvested, and the
money received from its sale could be invested elsewhere, if the owner so chooses.
If he decides to let the tree grow for another year or longer period, then the
interest he might have earned on this capital in another investment is a necessary

charge against the growing of more timber. The growing tree adds to its volume of wood, which usually means to its total value, and sometimes the added growth increases value more than proportionately to the increase in physical volume.

Wood growth per acre in a forest depends upon many natural factors such as soil and climate, and upon many management factors such as the density of the stand, the amount of fertilizer, and the nature of the thinnings. The growth of an individual tree also depends upon its age. Like any other living organism, a tree grows slowly in mass when it is very small, then grows more rapidly as an adolescent and young adult, with growth slowing down as maturity approaches, until in old age it does not grow at all and in time dies and decays. A forest established after a clearcut harvest or after a firm or storm has destroyed the former adult trees goes through somewhat similar age stages in growth, though the relationships are often more complex. A forest of mixed age trees, harvested at intervals, has still more complex growth, decay, and change relationships associated with age. The single tree reaches a physiological maturity at the point where its total mass is greatest; it reaches an economic maturity at a much earlier age, when its annual growth in value most exceeds the applicable interest rate or when its growth in value in relation to the value of the standing timber is the greatest, whichever is earlier. If no other factors were involved, economic maturity would be the rational time at which to harvest the tree.

Whatever is the age composition of the forest and whatever is the forest management program, substantial amounts of capital are necessarily tied up in the forest. But the amount of this capital is subject to management control within very wide limits, and the wise use of forest capital is an essential element in the wise management of any forest. Within a wide range of management alternatives, interest on capital tied up in standing timber is the major item of cost. As I have repeatedly emphasized, publicly owned forests should not be excused from the responsibility of earning interest on the capital value of their assets, or rent, when all the noncash outputs are valued at their most reasonable shadow price; and each method of management should earn at least as much, and preferably more, rent than its next best alternative management system.

The cost of capital for national forest management is arbitrarily set, with economic consequences more serious than those resulting from the arbitrary prices on some forest outputs. No charge is levied against national forest operations for use of the immense amount of capital tied up in them. In the budgeting-appropriation process in the Executive and Legislative Branches of the federal government, there are no calculations made as to a reasonable annual charge for use of this capital -- indeed, there is no discussion of the entire issue. The Forest Service is provided with an immense amount of interest-free capital, and is allowed, if not encouraged, to act as if there were no capital cost. Timber rotations and forest management practices which make good sense at zero interest rate rarely do so when a charge is made for use of capital.

The amount and form of new capital investment in roads, forest planting, and other improvements on the national forests are arrived at by a political rather than by an economic process. It may be argued that the Forest Service pays a political price for such investments, but no economic price is paid.

Numerous persons and groups have argued for the establishment of a capital account for the national forests. No private business charges to its annual operating costs the annual expenditures for capital investment and no public productive enterprise should do so. Separation of annual appropriations into management and investment would be highly desirable. But many of those who advocate establishment of a capital account do not seem to realize that a true capital account includes charges for the use of past capital investment.

In Table 8 the capital value of national forests was estimated at $42 billion, of which $20 billion was in standing timber. This is admittedly an approximation, but any reasonable estimate will show that a very large amount of capital is tied up in national forests, and hence a very large item of annual cost of national forest management is the interest on this capital. As has been pointed out earlier, the basic conclusions about use of capital in national forests are not changed if one assumes the capital there is only half the estimate used in Table 8; neither would they be changed if the estimate were double that figure. While there would be considerable gain from the best possible estimate of the present value of the national forests, the criticisms of present management and the suggestions for best future management do not depend upon the precise figure used in the analysis, if a figure somewhere within reason is actually chosen.

The real question is: is the amount of capital tied up in the national forests excessive by economic standards? More particularly, is the capital tied up in present volumes of standing timber excessive in relation to timber growth and harvesting? This question can be approached from either of two ways.

One may assume that forest industry firms have attempted to make an economically rational adjustment of the present value of the capital in standing timber on their forests. Their problem of optimum inventory in relation to output is similar to that of an oil company or a mining company which seeks an optimum reserve in relation to output, or even to that of a merchant who seeks an optimum relation of stock on shelves to sales. On this basis, the capital tied up in timber stands on national forests is excessive by about $12 billion.[26] That is, were national forest stands to be reduced to the level of stocking of

26/ Clawson, Forests for Whom and for What?, p. 101.

forest industry forests, the volume of timber so released could be sold for
$12 billion, even when generous allowance is made for the time required to
liquidate this excess inventory. It should be emphasized that this comparison
is based upon present capital tied up in timber stands per acre by forest industry firms; in no way does it include any investment on their part in timber
processing facilities, nor is it in any way dependent upon the historical costs
of their land and timber. Since forest industry firms were still in the process
of reducing their timber inventory per acre in 1970, it may be argued that even
their stocking rates were excessive by economic standards, so the $12 billion
would be a minimum figure.

The other approach is to assume that timber stands on national forests
are cut at their economically rational ages, and then to calculate the volumes
and values of the timber that would result from such a management program. By
use of data from the Forest Service, as well as other research, such calculations
can be made, at least approximately. This type of calculation will show that
the timber inventory on national forests is excessive by a larger amount than
will the former approach.

Regardless of the method of calculation, the conclusion is clear that the
present timber inventory in national forests is economically excessive. This
is an almost inevitable consequence of the fact that these forests still contain so much old growth timber, at very large volumes per acre of valuable
timber, on which the annual growth is low, zero, or even negative. It is un-
thinkable in modern America that the national forests be disposed of or the
timber liquidated without regrowth, but the volume of growing timber is within
management control and does not have to be at present levels. The large volumes
of old growth timber are growing slowly if at all; and rot, storm, disease, and
insect losses are high. As we noted in Table 5, mortality loss of sawtimber in

1970 was two-thirds as large as net growth. At the same time these forests are
growing so slowly, they lock up very large amounts of capital. On those commercial forests managed for timber production (that is, excluding substantial
acreages for wilderness, recreation, wildlife, and other values), a managed
rotation system in the future could produce far more wood every year at a vastly
smaller capital cost. It is ironic indeed that the national forests, where
appropriations for new investment expenditures are so low, should also contain
excessive idle capital. The national forests emerge as a great feudal estate,
land poor, managed extensively, relatively unproductive. It is difficult to
visualize any values resulting from the present capital intensive forest management that would not be available in equal or greater amount in a forest management program which economized on capital use.

If the excess timber inventory in national forests is $12 billion, then
the excess annual cost is $600 million at a 5 percent interest rate and higher
at interest rates current in the 1970s. The social significance of this excess
timber inventory becomes clearer if we realize that a national annual cost of
at least $600 million is equivalent to $3 per person. Anyone may imagine the
reaction that would ensue, were he to request each person in the United States,
individually, to contribute $3 annually to the maintenance of a very extensive
area of old growth forest, dominantly in rather remote locations in the West.
How many people would voluntarily pay this sum annually, to maintain a forest
they will likely never see and which they cannot even visualize? In making
this comparison, it must be emphasized again that it is excess inventory which
is in question. Substantial amounts of old growth timber would still exist and
the growing forests would be healthy and attractive, even were all the excess
removed. It should also be emphasized that the issue of this excess timber
inventory has nothing to do with the wilderness issue. Even if all the areas

which can even approximately approach the standards of wilderness were reserved for this purpose, the excess timber inventory issue would still remain on the areas where timber growing and timber harvest were practiced. The excess inventory on these lands could be harvested without disturbing the wilderness areas.

Functional Pattern of Investment and Operating Expenditures

The foregoing analyses strongly suggest that the functional pattern of investment in and operating expenditures on national forests is economically irrational. Timber management expenditures are made in regions or on forests or on sites where the timber values simply do not, and never will, justify them. At the same time, timber management and investment expenditures are too low in regions, forests, and sites where much larger expenditures would be economically sound. If adequate data were available, it might well be clear, at least in some regions, that expenditures on recreation and other outputs which do not produce cash income are too low in view of the probable value of the outputs. One cannot be certain to what extent operating and investment expenditures by functions are unwise, given the data and analytical deficiencies, but one strongly suspects much expenditure is in fact unwise. It may well be, as some Forest Service officials state, that progress in recognizing and dealing with this problem is being made within the agency, but there is yet a long way to go.

Management and Investment Expenditures by Forest Practices

It seems highly probable that some of the Forest Service's management practices are too costly in relation to results. A large part of the timber management expenditures are in connection with timber sales. The Forest Service, like other federal agencies, sells standing trees -- "stumpage." There is often not a competitive market for federal stumpage, in the economists' sense of the term, since the federal agency is the only or the dominant seller and since there are often so few buyers that each modifies his actions by his judgment of the probable response of his rivals.[27] But the law specifies that the timber shall be sold competitively, which means at bids. To avoid having a single bidder buying the timber at very low prices, the Forest Service makes elaborate timber appraisals, which then become the minimum acceptable bid for the stumpage. When there is active bidding the prices often go far above the appraised price. One major reason, in addition to any errors in the process, is that the appraisal price allows full depreciation of timber processing plant plus a reasonable profit margin; if hard pressed, a buyer can bid away much of this, and yet lose less money than if he failed to get the logs.

If the Forest Service, by employed labor force or by contract with loggers, were to cut its trees, transport them to a reasonably central place, and sell them by auction, the whole elaborate and expensive timber appraisal process could be avoided, better net prices could be obtained for the logs, and the agency would have better control over the methods of logging and their impact upon the environment. A few large timber firms in this country are beginning to trade logs at central markets, and selling of logs from public lands at roadside has long been practiced in some European countries.

The Forest Service has made timber sales on poor sites, where continued timber management is uneconomic, and has incurred costs for cleaning up the site (more for aesthetic than for silvicultural reasons) which were in excess of the value of the timber sold. It is difficult to justify timber management which costs more than it returns, especially since nontimber values are as likely to be reduced as to be increased thereby.

---

[27] Mead, Competition and Oligopsony in the Douglas-Fir Lumber Industry.

General Level of Annual Expenditures on National Forests

In fiscal year 1972 the total appropriations for national forest investment and management, when divided by the acreage of commercial forest within
the national forest system, resulted in a figure of $4.79 per acre (Table 10).
When other funds, notably those paid by forest users for rehabilitation of
forest harvest sites, were added, the figure was $6.53 per acre of commercial
forest. In the same year, the average expenditure per acre of 26 large forest
industry firms (nearly all the larger firms in the industry) for "forestry"
averaged $5.06 per acre of land owned or under control of the firm.[28] The
latter amount has been increasing rapidly in recent years, from $4.22 in 1970
to $6.42 in 1973, suggesting that these firms were finding it profitable to spend
more money in growing more wood in the forests they own or have under control. On
the face of it, these figures would suggest that the Forest Service is spending
somewhat more per acre of commercial forest in forest management than are the
larger private firms.

However, these figures are not wholly comparable, and adjustments must be
made for at least the following factors:

1. The national forest figures include expenditures on all lands within
the national forest system, and, as we saw earlier, only half of the acreage of
national forests is commercial forest. Eliminating the funds spent on nonforested areas or on forested areas of noncommercial forest would reduce the
national forest figure considerably. Although expenditures per acre on these
latter lands presumably are less, perhaps much less, than on the commercial
forest lands, their elimination would reduce the per acre figure of commercial

---

28/ I am indebted to William K. Condrell, General Counsel of the Forest Industry
Committee on Timber Valuation and Taxation, for these data. He is in no way responsible for my interpretation of the data, of course.

Table 10. Appropriations and Obligations From All Sources, All National Forests, Fiscal 1972

Item	Appropriations			Obligations, all sources of funds		
	Total (million dollars)	All land (dollars per acre of national forest)	Commercial forest (dollars per acre of national forest)	Total (million dollars)	All land (dollars per acre of national forest)	Commercial forest (dollars per acre of national forest)
Recreation and public use	40.3	.216	.438			
Wildlife habitat	6.2	.033	.067			
Range management and improvement	15.4	.082	.167	314.2	1.680	3.415
Timber management, sales, and reforestation	96.0	.513	1.043			
Miscellaneous	26.1	.140	.284			
Fire, insect, and disease control	49.6	.265	.539	59.0	0.316	0.641
Subtotal	233.6	1.249	2.539	373.2	1.996	4.057
Construction, land acquisition, roads and trails	206.8	1.106	2.248	227.8	1.218	2.476
TOTAL	440.4	2.355	4.786	601.0	3.214	6.533

Sources: Appropriations from Clawson, Forests for Whom and for What?, p. 142; Obligations from data provided by Forest Service; letter from John R. McGuire, July 17, 1975.

forest land at least to $5.00 per acre, perhaps considerably lower. The forest industry forest lands contain relatively little or no nonforested land.

2. The national forest figures include more expenditures for recreation, wildlife, watershed management, and other nontimber purposes than do the forest industry figures. These firms do spend some money for these purposes, but presumably considerably less, proportionately, than does the Forest Service. The national forest figure might be reduced as much as 20 percent, or to $4.00 per acre of commercial forest, by this adjustment, to get a figure which includes about the same range of activities as on the forest industry forests.

3. The national forest figure includes considerable expenditure for range management, whereas the forest industry figure includes very little for this purpose, but most of this adjustment has been made under point 1 above.

4. The national forest figure includes more nearly all the costs for fire protection, insect control, and disease control than do the forest industry figures. That is, other public funds pay a larger part of these costs on private land than on national forests. The extent of this adjustment is not large, but the national forest figures might be reduced by as much as 20 cents per acre to bring them to a comparable base with the industry figures.

5. The national forest figures include about 50 cents per acre of commercial forest for property acquisition, whereas the forest industry figures include nothing for this. To the extent that forest industry firms were acquiring forest property, those expenditures are reported elsewhere in their accounting systems. Both sets of figures include costs of building timber access roads, although possibly not to the same degree or to the same standard of roads.

6. The national forest figures include considerable outlays necessary for timber sales, including timber cruises, timber valuations, sales preparation

and advertising, and sale supervision. As noted previously, the Forest Service must sell its timber to private buyers, whereas the forest industry managers are not faced with this problem. Some of the data-gathering and planning done by the Forest Service would also be done by a well-managed private firm but some of these expenses could be avoided. The costs that might be avoided by not making timber sales have been estimated at nearly half the Forest Service timber management expenditures.[29/] The data in Table 11 seem to support an adjustment of at least 50 cents per acre of commercial forest in the national forest figures, to make them more nearly comparable with forest industry figures.

7. Contrary to all the foregoing adjustments, which would reduce national forest figures to make them more nearly comparable to forest industry figures, an adjustment must be made for the fact that the national forest figures in Table 11 do _not_ include any payments out of revenue to the counties, whereas the forest industry figures include a substantial sum for taxes.

The analysis in this section leads to the conclusion that the _general level_ of timber management expenditures on national forests is _not_ too high, and may well be too low. The real criticisms of national forest timber management, developed in earlier sections, is that the money is spent in the wrong places and for the wrong activities. If the adjustments implicit in these criticisms were made, and the available funds spent on more economical sites and for more economically justifiable activities, then national forest expenditures might be adequate, or more nearly adequate than they now appear.

Two caveats must immediately be made about these data and this conclusion drawn from them: (1) this analysis is entirely in terms of timber management, and says nothing about the level of national forest expenditures for other

_____

29/ I am indebted to Lawrence W. Libby for some umpublished figures which form the basis of this statement. The interpretation is mine, not Libby's.

Table 11. Adjustment of Reported National Forest Expenditures
on Forest Management to Comparable Basis with
Forest Industry Expenditures

Item	Amount of adjustment ($ per acre)	Resulting figure ($ per acre)
Reported total expenditure (Table 10)		6.53
Adjustment for:		
1. Expenditures on nonforest areas and range management	1.53	5.00
2. Greater expenditures on nontimber outputs	1.00	4.00
3. Range Management Expenditures	a/	4.00
4. Public sharing of costs of fire, insect, and disease control	0.20	3.80
5. Property acquisition costs	0.50	3.30
6. Cost of making timber sales	0.50	2.80
7. Payments in lieu of taxes - add	0.70	3.50
Comparable forest industry figure		5.06

a/ Included in item 1.

purposes, such as recreation -- the Forest Service has always estimated the
need for funds for these purposes as higher than the actual appropriations,
and conservationists have nearly always agreed; and (2) this analysis says
nothing about the efficiency with which the Forest Service uses the funds
available to it. A low level of expenditures might mean high efficiency or
it might mean inadequate management, and a high level of expenditures might
mean inefficiency or it might mean intensive management.

The Results of Arbitrary Prices

Many of the outputs from national forests are priced arbitrarily, at far
below their reasonable value. Outdoor recreation is available at low prices,
sometimes zero prices, as is wilderness opportunity. Wildlife and watershed
values are mostly not priced at all. There is no pretense in the national
forest regulations and management that these goods and services are made available at their full economic value. The lack of reasonable prices distorts the
production and consumption decisions on these products and services, and materi-
ally affects the distribution of income from their use, as noted previously.

In the management of the national forests, the Forest Service, the Secretary of Agriculture, the Office of Management and Budget, and the Congress lack
any measure of the real values of these goods and services, hence lack any measure of justifiable costs to produce them. The arguments for and against appropriations for the production of these goods and services must therefore rest on other
grounds. It is difficult to make rational choices in the absence of the necessary data. Are enough, or too much, or too little funds being spent for watershed
management, provision of outdoor recreation, reservation of wilderness areas, and
the like? Are the available funds spent in the right or the wrong places, and
for the right mix of outputs? Our analysis for timber management has been unavoidably less specific, less accurate, less definitive than would be desirable;

but the analysis for any of the other outputs of the national forests is, by comparison, infinitely worse.

Some of this uncertainty could be reduced, if not avoided, by the use of shadow prices. In an earlier section, "shadow prices" were defined as the best estimates of what prices actually would be if there were free trading in a reasonably competitive market. At the best, they are estimates of what does not actually exist, hence they can never be free of a degree of uncertainty and perhaps of argument. At the lowest level of sophistication of analysis, a shadow price is estimated and is multiplied by the reported volume of transactions or activities, to yield an estimated total value of output. At a somewhat more advanced level of analysis, recognition is given to the fact that a price or a charge would affect the volume of transactions or activities; an estimate of the reduced volume is made, and the shadow price applied to it, to calculate total value. At still a more advanced stage of analysis, the effect of higher (or lower) total expenditures for the commodity or service in question is calculated for expenditures on other commodities and services, and the repercussions from this substitution played back into their effect upon prices and volume of the commodity or service under study. In Table 8, shadow prices were, in effect, applied to outdoor recreation and to wilderness, on the lowest or primary level of sophistication outlined above. That is, the reported volume of recreation visits were multiplied by $2.00 each to get a total value of outdoor recreation, and the reported number of wilderness visits was multiplied by $10.00 to get a total value of wilderness experience. These shadow prices were very rough approximations, without elaborate analysis to back them up. They did not take into account the effect such prices would have upon volume of visits.

By the best, but unavoidably rough, methods, shadow prices could be estimated for each of the goods and services produced from national forests that are

now available at prices far below their values. Some progress has been made
in this direction, and a larger effort could yield much larger results. In
the absence of such estimates, the values of these outputs is often ignored,
which in effect means that a zero value has been placed on them. Others will
argue that some of these values are so great that all management must be directed
toward their preservation or production, which in effect means an infinitely
large value has been placed on such goods and services. Neither extreme is
defensible or helpful in actual management decisions. It is often objected that
accurate values cannot be placed on many of these goods and services; as noted
previously, however, there is no way that managers, public officials, and the
general electorate can avoid placing values on them. The real issues turn on
the care, objectivity, and accuracy with which such estimates are made.

Shadow prices could help substantially in the making of management decisions for the production of the goods and services here under discussion.
They would enable each of the actors in the appropriation and management
process to compare the gains from expenditures of funds for one output with
another, for one location with another, and for one method of operation with
another. Shadow prices would not significantly help consumers make more rational
choices, for consumption decisions rest primarily on prices actually paid. A
good case could be made for charging prices for some national forest outputs
that more nearly approximated full values of the goods and services.

If shadow prices were estimated for recreation, wilderness, wildlife,
watershed, and other goods and services now available at less than full value,
this would throw a spotlight on the equity problems created by such arbitrary
prices. The beneficiaries of such arbitrary prices would be more visible, and
their gains would be less defensible than is the case now, when the values concerned are less accurately known. The increased visibility of the equity

problem may well be one of the reasons why some of the beneficiaries of such arbitrary prices oppose attempts to estimate the values concerned.

Less readily apparent than the arbitrary prices on some national forest outputs, but at least as pernicious in its effects, is the arbitrary price on capital used in national forest management. As we have noted, no charge is made for the enormous amount of capital tied up in timber stands, land, and other assets of the national forests. The Forest Service is encouraged to operate as if the cost of capital was zero and as if the economic rent of its land and forests was zero. Its long rotations, its heavy stands of timber, and its practices on unproductive sites are all natural consequences of this lack of a capital charge. If the Forest Service had to pay even a modest interest rate (5 percent or less) on the capital embodied in the national forests, even the most virulently antieconomics forester would be forced to reexamine his operations. In a modern era, in which capital in all forms and for all purposes is limited, and in which capital for public enterprises is particularly scarce, the existence of a vast store of free capital, producing only a miniscule return (even when nonpriced outputs are valued generously), is intolerable.

Environmental Measures and National Forest Management

The Forest Service is one of the oldest, strongest, and best known of the public resource and conservation agencies. It pioneered in such concepts as multiple use, sustained yield, and conservation for seventy-five years. Its programs for forest and range management have been developed with these broad concepts as a basis.

The rise of the modern popular environmental movement has challenged the Forest Service in many ways. The Forest Service is now required to justify to other federal agencies many of the management decisions and actions

which long had been its exclusive responsibility. It must prepare and make
public, and publicly explain and defend, many decisions which previously had
been made by its own processes within the agency. It has increasingly been
challenged by private parties who have instituted lawsuits against it. Its
expertise in its traditional fields has been downgraded and even denied.

Attitudes toward this changed state of affairs differ greatly. At one
extreme are those who feel that the new laws and the lawsuits merely force
the Forest Service to do what it should have done all along, and merely require that the agency obey the law. To those who hold this view, the environmental measures would not be a real burden if the Forest Service genuinely
sought to respect them. At the other extreme are those who regard the recent
environmental measures as an added burden on the Forest Service, which take
manpower away from essential tasks, reduce national forest output, and add
to national forest management costs, including delays in implementing management decisions. Many others have attitudes intermediate between these ex-
tremes.

This report will not attempt a full assessment of the impact of environmental requirements on national forest management. The subject is a complex
one, about which quick judgments are likely to be at least partially in error.
All the facts one would need for an assessment are not in hand. It does seem
fairly clear that, if the environmental measures are merely layered on to the
old ways of national forest planning and management, then additional costs and
serious delays will occur. The real questions seem to be, how far and how
well can environmental concerns be worked into Forest Service processes at
less added cost, with less delay, and, it is hoped, with better all-around
results? Could some of the conflict among the Environmental Protection Agency,
Forest Service, forest industry, environmentalists, preservationists, and

others be replaced by a more cooperative approach among these and perhaps other parties? The present situation does not seem very satisfactory to anyone. New approaches are greatly needed and these may require new attitudes.

Regional and Local Impacts of National Forest Management

The main focus of this report has been on the national, as contrasted with the regional and local, aspects of national forest management. A truly comprehensive analysis of the economics of national forest management would necessarily include a consideration of these more localized impacts. Separate analyses, which started at the regional or local level, and were contained within the framework of a national analysis, would be desirable. We have noted that the national forests are concentrated in some regions of the United States, in the West particularly. Their regional and local impacts will clearly be greater where they are a large part of the land area and forest resource than where they are more limited.

Introduction of more economics into national forest management would have marked regional and local economic effects. The thrust of the analysis in this report has been that timber management is uneconomic under many national forest situations. Transforming that timber management into an economically more rational one would greatly reduce, if not eliminate, all timber management in some regions, notably the Rocky Mountain and Eastern regions. Likewise, if some of the other outputs of national forests were brought within some kind of an economic rationale, they might be decreased in some regions and increased in others.

One problem of making regional changes in national forest management is that many private businesses, often small but important locally, are dependent upon national forest outputs. This is most marked with small sawmills, which

depend entirely or almost entirely upon national forest timber. A considerable
number of such small industries exist in the Rocky Mountain areas but are not
unknown elsewhere. Outfitters for wilderness parties and suppliers of recreation equipment and services (including guides) are also dependent upon national
forest outputs. If economic analysis resulted in a cutting back of national
output locally, this could be serious to such local businesses. This is one
of several places where Forest Service planning should involve local people
deeply. A continued uneconomic operation of a national forest function is a
form of national subsidy to a local area. While subsidies are very common in
the national economy, question can always be raised as to the degree of national
interest in such local subsidy.

Financial Outlook

If the potential outputs of the national forests, as shown in Table 7,
were to be achieved, and if the economies inherent in the foregoing criticisms
were made, what would the financial outlook then be for the national forest
system? A precise answer is impossible because of many uncertainties. If the
timber inventory were reduced to the economically rational point, if timber
management were abandoned on the low productive sites (Site Class V and maybe
others), and if major economies were achieved by simplified management, substantial savings in annual operating costs could be achieved -- in terms of the price
level of Table 8, perhaps $700 to $1,000 million annually. At the same time,
cash income could be doubled or more, also in terms of the same price level, by
selling a great deal more timber each year and the value (if not the cash income)
of the services and products sold for less than full value would be increased
greatly, as more of these services became available.

On the other hand, all this could be achieved only by much greater expenditures on the sites best for each kind of use. Shifting management emphasis to economic locations, methods, and functions for each kind of output would free much appropriated money for more intensive management of the sites best for each use. Even at the best, one would expect total expenditures to rise -- intensive forest management means greater inputs per unit of area.

It seems unlikely that the national forests can be made to earn as much as 5 percent interest even on a reduced timber inventory, and it might not be above 3 percent. While this seems low, it is vastly above the 1/2 of 1 percent presently earned. It almost surely could be a lot higher on the more productive sites. All of these comparisons give full value to all outputs of the forest, whether sold for cash or not. The national forests can never be made into a big money earner for the benefit of the American taxpayer -- too much of their output is given away or sold at nominal prices.

The big economic return to the nation, if the national forests were managed to achieve their potential, would not be money paid into the Treasury, but more goods and services flowing into the economy, at reasonable prices, and more services for the benefit of the whole population.

6. What Is Wrong with the National Forest Management Record?

A present production of every kind of output from the national forests so far below the economic potential and at such an excessive cost is a poor record. Even when all outputs made available to the public or to parts of it at minimum prices are evaluated at their full economic value, the return on the huge capital value of the national forests is but 1/2 of 1 percent. A resource management record of this kind is unacceptable for either privately or publicly owned natural resources. More serious than the record of the recent past is the danger that the future performance will be equally bad unless positive measures are taken to change it.

The positive values of the national forests and of the Forest Service are great and must be weighed against their deficiencies in any balanced analysis. The reservation of large areas of public domain and the purchase of substantial areas of formerly private land for permanent public ownership and management has been a desirable aspect of modern American life. The Forest Service has made great contributions to American forestry and has pioneered in many ways. The issue is not whether the national forest management and the Forest Service have been "bad" or "good" in some absolute sense, but is rather whether they have each been as good as the nation has a right to expect. In this relative sense, their record is unsatisfactory. Why has this been so?

The problem is a complex one, and no single factor is responsible for the results. Perhaps no two critics would cite exactly the same factors. Without trying to weigh the respective force of each deficiency or even to rank the importance of the various factors, a number of somewhat separate yet closely interrelated factors or causes may be listed.

Who Is Responsible?

As one views the record of national forest management, a natural question is: Who is responsible for the poor results? This question might be asked as part of a search for a culprit, or it might be asked in a genuine search for future improvement. It is raised here in the latter spirit.

Clearly, the Forest Service, as the agency directly in charge of the national forests, has some measure of responsibility for the results. But, equally clearly, it is not the only organization involved. One can identify three other major agencies or organizations, as well as perhaps several less directly involved: the Department of Agriculture, the Office of Management and Budget, and the Congress. The last has several committees whose concerns and actions involve the national forests. The responsibility for the national forests is divided among these four groups (including the Forest Service as one), and it is by no means easy to allocate the responsibility among them.

For instance, how far has the Forest Service actually been constrained by the Congress in any national forest management matter, such as, for instance, the allocation of funds by site classes? How far does the Forest Service think it is constrained by the Congress? The language of appropriations and other acts is one thing, the sentiment in the Congress or in the committee may be another; what is legally possible may not be politically possible. How far has the Congress been constrained in its actions by what it thinks the Forest Service can and will do in some matter? How far is the attitude of the Congress based upon actual actions of the Forest Service and how far upon its beliefs of what the Forest Service will do, which in turn rested upon the agency's beliefs about what the Congress will do? These examples could be multiplied many times. In particular, the role of OMB and of the Secretary of Agriculture should be considered; the more actors, the greater the number of interrelations, primary, secondary, and so on.

Even the most searching research or investigative inquiry might leave these questions partially unanswered. A mere review of the public record would be insufficient. The intangible but governing factor of the beliefs of the actors, especially their evaluation of one another, is most unlikely to be spread upon the public record but may be decisive. It has been impossible in the present study to pursue these matters as far as one would like. This report presents the record of what actually took place, as far as that is possible and as far as it seems relevant; it could not explore the matter of motivations, attitudes, and decision processes.

Foresters' Attitudes

Foresters as a professional group and the Forest Service as the agency managing the national forests have emphasized "silvicultural considerations," "multiple use," "sustained yield," "community stability," and other relatively undefined (at least to an economist) terms, while at the same time rejecting economic considerations or economic analysis as applied to the national forests. To most foresters in the Forest Service, the quoted phrases in the preceding sentence were good things, almost articles of faith, not to be tested or challenged. There has been a special emphasis upon long periods for conversion of old growth stands to managed rotations. The extensive loss of timber during these long conversion periods and the very high capital costs of massive inventories of low-producing timber are ignored or brushed aside. Foresters employed by private firms have been forced to think in new terms, but public foresters still seem to ignore economics and the interest rate.

The management of national forests by the Forest Service has been very much an ingrown forester-dominated process. The Forest Service has typically recruited young men who started at the bottom, worked their way up the bureaucratic ladder, and spent their entire professional lives at the agency. In former times, very few foresters left the Forest Service because alternate professional employment opportunities were limited. In more recent times, a somewhat higher percentage of those entering the service have left for employment elsewhere. But there has never been any significant recruitment of national forest managers at any level except the beginning one. The Forest Service has done an extraordinary job of inculcating its men with the organization's ideals and standards, so that men working by themselves, facing difficult problems on the ground, could each individually take decisions which were very much within the spirit and practice of the whole organization.[30/] While this has many desirable results, it does tend to reduce dissent, innovation, and the intro- duction of wholly new approaches. Men on higher rungs of the ladder tend to face their problems in ways they learned during their early days and during their ascent of that ladder.[31/] The early dedication to multiple use, sustained yield, long timber rotations, maintenance of community stability, and the other standards of value and of conduct has tended to make the Service less flexible to meet new problems or to attempt new solutions to old problems. The high pro- fessionalism of the Forest Service has always been an asset but it has made difficult the accommodation to the views of outsiders, whether those outsiders were in other federal agencies or in the general public. Many men in the Forest Service today will acknowledge the necessity of greater public involvement in national forest planning and in operations, yet be at a loss to see how this can be done within their traditional framework of agency analysis, debate, and decision making.

Free or Nearly Free Use National Forest Outputs

The fact that so many of the outputs of the national forests are free or at prices far below their values makes for exaggeration of those values and for waste of those resources, as we have noted. Careful economic analysis is, at the best, difficult when important values are so hard to measure. The situation

---

30/ Herbert Kaufman, The Forest Ranger: A Study in Administrative Behavior, Baltimore: Johns Hopkins University Press for Resources for the Future, 1960.

31/ Ibid. One of the district rangers Kaufman interviewed in 1958 was Rexford A. Resler, now Associate Chief of the Forest Service. Nearly all top administrators of the Forest Service have worked their way up through the ranks.

also makes for controversies, where assertions take the place of data and reasoned analysis. The advocate of wilderness, or the wildlife spokesman, or the irrigation district official, or the recreation specialist, can each argue for the value of the output he is interested in, even though none can provide reliable quantitative data, and the Forest Service is forced to make decisions on the allocation of resources without dependable knowledge of the values involved in each competing use. This factor, in combination with others, surely makes more likely a wastage of capital and an inefficiency in management.

Faced with demands from the beneficiaries of these outputs priced at less than their value, the Forest Service has often and naturally sought to mitigate the controversies by provision of some of the services demanded. Available appropriations have typically been less than adequate to provide all such services, in part because the lack of imputed price and income data have given the decision makers in the appropriation process no basis for judgment as to the socially optimum level of appropriations. The result has frequently been that available funds have been spread thinly, that the attempt has been made to provide some of these services everywhere, and that, therefore, the Service has been unable to provide them adequately where it would have been economically justifiable to do so.

The lack of usable estimates of the value of these unpriced outputs of the national forests would not, alone, have been decisive in producing the kind of national forest management analyzed in earlier pages of this study. But, taken together with the several other factors listed in this section, it surely has been an influential force.

Federal Budget-Appropriation-Expenditure Process

The federal budget-appropriation-expenditure process was developed for governmental and social services, not for public enterprises producing economic output.[32] This is an old story but it cannot be emphasized too much. The process is too slow, too cumbersome, too unresponsive to changed conditions, and discourages the long-term planning, investment, and management which is so important for forestry. Too little attention is given to output and to the relation between costs and value of output. Too often, expenditures postponed have been regarded as "savings," regardless of loss of income today or tomorrow, and often regardless of the fact that larger expenditures will be required in the future because of today's "savings." The process has many actors, each of whom can throw sand in the gears, none of whom can guarantee that the process will work, and none of whom will or can take full responsibility for ensuring success.

Lack of Clear Legislative Directive

The Forest Service has never had a clear legislative directive to guide it in its management of the national forests. For a long time the Forest Service operated under the antiquated language of the 1897 Act regarding the sale of forest products from the national forests; it thought it had Congressional approval for its adaptation of the language of the act to meet modern conditions, but in recent years the courts have overthrown this accommodation. The Multiple Use and Sustained Yield Act of 1960, which the Forest Service sought and which at least in large part embodied its concepts, gave a somewhat firmer legislative base for many necessary decisions by the agency, but it did not provide a clear policy guide. As noted earlier in this report, the Forest Service accepted some, but not too much, economizing as its goal. The 1960 act, or others, might have adopted a different approach, by directing the Forest Service to produce specified

---

32/ Clawson and Held, The Federal Lands.

kinds and amounts of products and services from the national forests at the
minimum costs, but no act has done this. The language of the 1960 act provides
guidelines in general phrases, subject to many interpretations, and without
a clear standard for judgment.

The lack of clear legislative directive for national forest management
directly reflects the lack of a clear national consensus for these lands and
forests. Various groups in the total population want different things from
the national forests, and each naturally enough tries to get what it wants.
The divergent views or objectives have not been resolved in the legislative
or political arena. Instead, the problems have been bucked down to the Forest
Service, which has had no clear signal, no solid basis for its decisions.

Partly as a result of the foregoing, and partly as a result of other
factors, the Forest Service in recent years, at all levels from the chief's
office down to the district ranger, has all too often seemed confused and
uncertain as to its own course, as to the best way to deal with the cross-
currents which have buffeted it. Controversy surely is not new to the Forest
Service -- it was born in controversy, and its first chief, Gifford Pinchot,
actively sought controversy as he fought for his ideals and ambitions. Throughout its long history, the Forest Service has been engaged in many controversies.
The distinguishing aspect of its more recent history has been that it seemed to
be uncertain how to deal with the controversial problems surrounding national
forest management.

Lack of Economic Tests

In the past there have been no economic tests of national forest management. The lack of such tests in the appropriation process has been noted previously. But economics has not been the basis for allocation of available appropriations among regions or forests or specific localities within forests. Nor has

it been the basis for decisions upon forest functions or management practices. Even now, many foresters in the Forest Service explicitly reject such tests as applied to national forest management. There are some faint stirrings of economic analysis in the Forest Service, more in its research than in its operating branch, but these have not yet really entered the blood stream of management policy. The Congress has been dissatisfied with the forest output and management situation, and the Humphrey-Rarick Act of 1974, which might well provide a vehicle for careful and thorough consideration of forestry, not only in the national forests but outside of them, is as yet untested.

Lawrence W. Libby, as a result of his studies of decision making for forests, is convinced that effective implementation of the Humphrey-Rarick Act will require a new act of management incentives for the man in the field.[33] The man down the line in the Forest Service is often not convinced that this kind of planning will gain him anything he wants for the management of his area, or for himself personally. Compliance with directives is one thing, adoption of a new process as an integral part of mental operations, forest planning, and day-to-day operations is quite another thing.

The basic problem is the philosophical or attitudinal one noted above; good machinery for governmental decision making will help, but it is unlikely to be sufficient. Unless or until national forest managers are willing to apply economic tests to all aspects of their operations, including their expenditures in relation to their results, the management of the national forests will continue at lower levels of output and lower levels of efficiency than are reasonably attainable.

33/ Lawrence W. Libby, unpublished studies.

Multiple Use in Practice

All too often in national forest management, "multiple use" has meant a little of everything everywhere, regardless of costs and of results. The tendency to invest too much capital in poor sites, at the expense of more rewarding investment on better sites, the tendency to practice timber management on sites where timber cannot be grown economically, and other similar actions have been noted. Each national forest supervisor and ranger has wanted a diversified program. He has especially wanted to include timber management in his territory, fearing that in its absence his work would not be properly appreciated or that the funds available to him would be inadequate. Many forest rangers feel that they need a timber management program to justify the staff and equipment they deem necessary in their district, and the costs and returns of that timber management are unimportant to them. In many cases, intangible but powerful forces of personal prestige and of peer evaluation are also involved. Many foresters feel that somehow they are not fully respected foresters unless they have some timber operations going -- that being merely recreation foresters, or watershed foresters, or wildlife foresters would not earn them the regard of their forester peers.

There has been a notable lack within the Forest Service of an organization-wide or region-wide approach to multiple use, as contrasted with a localized approach. That is, one searches in vain for statements of Forest Service policy which say that multiple use for the agency or for the region may mean no activity at all of some kind in extensive areas, and more intensive application of that activity elsewhere. Here again, the ingrown orientation of the Forest Service management personnel is a serious factor.

Responsibility of the General Public and of
Conservation Organizations

Lastly, in all of this the general user public of the national forests, and especially the conservation organizations, cannot avoid some responsibility for the uneconomic management of the national forests. Public concern has all too often been badly misplaced, and the potentials for achieving greater outputs of all kinds and thus of reconciling conflicts have been ignored or passed over. The general public has often been indifferent to national forests, leaving the subject to the parties at interest. In this, of course, the national forests are not unique; the situation of general public neglect and of interested party participation is a common one.

But one can scarcely be encouraged or satisfied with the role that the "conservation" organizations have played in the management of the national forests. All too often, they have acted more like private interest groups, than like the public interest advocates they claim to be. They have given most of their attention to specific and sometimes unimportant management or local issues, such as clearcutting or a specific wilderness area, rather than attempting to view the forests as a whole. At times, they seem to have been more interested in headlines than in results. The general problems of national forests, and more explicitly the great potentials of the forests to satisfy all needs and demands, seem not to have had their serious attention. In all this, the role of the information media has also been disappointing. Naturally enough, they have played up controversy, but in the process they have often contributed little to understanding of basic issues and of real possibilities. Misinformation from information media is not uncommon. A reporter may stress the "overcutting" of national forests in a region, paying no attention to the missed opportunities for greater timber growth, for instance.

One cannot, of course, hold the general public, the conservation interests, or the information media fully responsible for either the positive aspects of national forest management or for the deficiencies in that management. However, if the potentials of the national forests to meet the needs of the American people are to be achieved, a larger concern and a wider constituency than the economic interest groups or the professional foresters is urgently needed.

7. How To Achieve the National Forest Potential

If a strong national effort were made to achieve the potential of the national forests to provide the maximum economically attainable volume of wood, wilderness, wildlife, water, and outdoor recreation, what are the minimum components of such an effort?

Just as the causes of the present unsatisfactory state of national forest affairs are complex, as described in the preceding section, so the measures to achieve the potential must be diverse, somewhat complicated, and interrelated. There is no single simple remedy to a complex situation such as the national forests present today. Even combined measures can fail if one or more elements are missing or are weak.

Before describing the improvement measures needed, a short review of what is at stake may be helpful. The data in Table 7 show that the national forests can grow economically more than twice as much wood as they now grow, and a larger percentage of that increased growth can be harvested annually; they can provide a designated area of wilderness nearly four times the present designated wilderness area; they can provide more than twice as much outdoor recreation as they now provide; somewhat more wildlife can find a home on the national forests; and the volume of water flowing off them can be increased modestly -- all this, in

combination, at the same time, and all reasonably economically. These added
volumes of goods and services can contribute significantly to the quality of
American life -- can help provide more housing at lower prices, more recreation for those interested in it, and so forth. Some of these gains, as in
a more ample wood supply, will benefit everyone in our society. The total
value of the increased outputs could well be more than $1 billion annually --
an important sum, even for the United States today.

At the same time, it is necessary to preserve some perspective. A
failure of national forests to produce as much as they economically can will
lower the quality of American life, but it will not threaten the national
existence or even the national well-being. The future of the United States
as an independent country does not depend upon the output of the national
forests. Even without their output, or with their output at present levels,
people would have some kind of housing, albeit somewhat more expensively
than otherwise, and would have paper products, also more expensive than otherwise. There are many other aspects of the American economy and social struc-
ture which are more basic than are national forests. They are important, and
their efficient management is a matter of national concern, but one cannot
seriously argue that they are critical.

National Leadership

An alert, intelligent, concerned, continuous national leadership is
basic for adequate management of national forests. The President must have
some realization of what the national forests are, what their present problems
and deficiencies are, and of what is needed. Obviously, with the very great

international and domestic problems requiring presidential attention in the
United States, no President, no matter how concerned he might be about
national forests, could devote much time to them. But his choice of staff,
his insistence on results, and his continued overall supervision are critical.

The first place where a topflight lieutenant of the President is
needed is in the Office of Management and Budget. A truly senior person
really interested and concerned about national forests, imaginative and
constructive rather tham negative in attitude. and with continued attention
to the national forests for some years will be needed if the constructive
ideas of any President are not to be buried. Although there is no place
in this report for a detailed evaluation of the OMB senior staff, there is
reason to believe, if only because of continued turnover, that it has func-
tioned inadequately. Good, concerned, dedicated staff at junior levels in
OMB will not make up the deficiencies of junior staff.

The Secretary of Agriculture must also have some genuine concern about
the national forests, some imagination and some willingness to innovate,
and be attentive to the Forest Service, but not its captive. The relationship between the Secretary of Agriculture and the Forest Service is a difficult and complex one. On the one hand, the Secretary must depend upon the
Service's technical competence and he must support it in the carrying out
of Administration policies, however difficult and controversial this may be
at times. He cannot substitute his political objectives for its reasoned
resource management decisions without severe damage to the agency and to its
programs. On the other hand, the Secretary should not be a captive of the
Service, uncritically accepting its every request, never questioning its
analyses and its programs.

There has been a severe dearth of executive branch leadership for the Forest Service and the national forests in recent years. Congress, or at least some members of Congress, have sought to provide some of the lacking leadership. The Forest and Rangeland Renewable Resources Planning Act of 1974 was one such effort. But Congress suffers serious handicaps in trying to fill the gap left by a weak executive, on any matter. Congress, too, must adopt some new attitudes toward the national forests, if their full potential is to be achieved. Requests for appropriations must be considered with great care, but also with genuine willingness to make appropriations on a fully justified scale. The earlier parts of this report have outlined some of the necessary features of optimum national forest appropriations. If there is to be a wider public constituency for the national forests, with less unquestioned acceptance of the position of the interest groups which politically support a member. then the Congress must bestir itself on national forest matters.

New Procedures and Analyses

New procedures and new analyses of national forest operations are necessary. The Forest and Rangeland Renewable Resources Planning Act will help, but it is doubtful if it is fully adequate and in any case it is as yet untested. The kinds of questions asked in this report must be asked within the Forest Service at all levels from the ranger district to the national headquarters, within the Department, at OMB, and in the Congress. They must be asked about every activity at every site classification; what are the gains, what are the costs, are the gains worth the costs, and who bears costs and who gets the gains? What better alternatives exist? Such questions must be asked and answers sought honestly and earnestly, but at reasonable cost in time and money. Had such questions been asked sharply enough in the past, the efficiency of national forest management today would have been vastly higher than it is.

Some means must be developed for the making of wise decisions about national forest management and then some means provided for actually carrying out the decisions reached. Forestry is a long-term investment and management enterprise, and some means must be found to work out long-range plans which can be reexamined and modified at intervals but which in the main are carried out. The Forest Service must have some real assurance of funding levels over a period of time; annual appropriations without a long-range commitment, no matter how generous they are, do not provide an adequate basis for truly constructive national forest management. Not only must available funds be adequate to carry out agreed-upon plans, but they must be available when needed. Some means of speeding up the normal budgeting and appropriation process is necessary.

Some means must be found for linking operating and investment outlays to expected results (including values of nonpriced as well as priced outputs) and of rejecting management plans which do not offer real prospects of favorable net results. This could be done entirely at the analytical or planning level, if such plans were examined critically by the Congress and implemented by appropriations when the results were favorable. It could also be done by some means of actually linking expenditures to income, including among the latter the values of services made available at less than full value. This would subject the operations of the national forests to the discipline of the marketplace, or at least to the decisions of national forest users. Various proposals to this end have been made in the past and have always been opposed by conservation groups who feared that timber would overwhelm other outputs of the forest in the competition for funds. If appropriations were geared to total values of all outputs, not merely to cash values of some outputs, some of this concern might disappear.

Various means could be devised to provide financial continuity and assurance, both in amount and in timing. One would be the use of cash receipts, or part of them, plus appropriations geared to values of noncash outputs, as the financial base for all national forest operations. This would surely arouse concern and opposition from many quarters, but it would have great management value. Some sort of revolving fund might meet the timing problem. Something like this has been done for forest fire fighting for many years; fires are fought and the costs paid for out of any available funds, and supplementary appropriations later make good the funds concerned. A commitment from the Administration and from the Congress, such as the Forest and Rangeland Renewable Resources Planning Act envisages, for continued financial support to a fully justified level, might provide the answers, if such commitment is really honored over the years.

This report is not the place for a detailed consideration of the various financing and management alternatives for the national forests, but the most serious, imaginative, and comprehensive review of the whole process of national forest management and finance is urgently needed. The alternatives come in many forms and degrees of change from the present: at the minimum, more economics in Forest Service planning and budgeting; at the next layer of change, more economic scrutiny of national forest appropriations and operations at every executive and congressional level above the Forest Service; at another and greater level of change, some form of direct relationship between expenditures and values created thereby; and lastly, some form of public corporation, which had to live within the confines of the values it created.$\underline{34}$/

Forest Service Personnel Changes

A massive infusion of new blood into the Forest Service is essential, if the national forests are to achieve their economic potential. In a situation where a federal program is not satisfactory, a typical proposal is to get a new head of the agency. This would certainly not be sufficient, and may not be necessary or desirable in the present case. No chief of the Forest Service, no matter what his background, his aims and ideals, and no matter what he tried to do, can succeed in significantly new approaches to national forest management, without a lot of new blood. One strategy might be to let normal aging and attrition provide the opportunities for new recruitment; but this is slow and it may largely perpetuate the past, as in fact it has largely done until now in the Forest Service.

A significant infusion of new blood--on the order of a third of the total management staff--at all levels of the Forest Service seems necessary. The new people should come from conservation groups, from the forest industry, and a significant proportion from wholly outside of forestry. Technical skills are relatively unimportant in this new blood infusion, for they exist within the present Forest Service staff; new attitudes, new approaches, more emphasis upon management analyses and techniques, and above all more economics or more business (whichever term you prefer) are necessary if the kinds of questions raised in this report are to be asked insistently and if the kinds of potentials outlined here are to be achieved.

$\underline{34}$/ Clawson and Held, The Federal Lands, pp. 347-362.

The Forest Service has long been praised as an outstanding public agency
and in many ways it still is, but its achievements are in the past and its past
skills are not sufficient for today's problems. A proposal to reshape the
Forest Service drastically will disturb, even outrage, many of its friends.
But few thoughtful friends have been satisfied with the organization's performance in recent years, and a shaping with a friendly motive may be preferable to one with unfriendly intent.

A Concluding Comment

This report has unavoidably dealt only with highlights; time and manpower available to the author have not permitted detailed consideration of
many matters, and data deficiencies would in any case have constrained the
analysis. The approach has been critical but friendly. The national forests
are a great national asset, but they are poorly managed. There are great
possibilities to make them the source of much greater outputs of all kinds,
and to make their operations economically far more efficient at the same time.
Creation of the Forest Service seventy years ago was one of the great imaginative innovations of the natural resource field; its reconstitution and re-
direction could be the single greatest conservation achievement of the latter
half of the 20th century.